SMALL STATES SYNDROME IN INDIA

About the Author

Dr. B.B. Kumar, M.Sc. (Double), M.A., Ph.D. (*b.* 1941) is the Ex-Principal, Science College, Kohima. He was a member, Executive Council, Academic Council & University Court, North Eastern Hill University, Shillong.

He remained associated with a large number of academic and voluntary bodies from time to time during the last 22 years, such as, founder Secretary, Nagaland Bhasha Parishad; Thinkers Forum, Nagaland; Council for Social Service, Nagaland; Founder President, Educational Society of Nagaland, Nagaland College Principals Forum and All Nagaland Govt. College Teachers Association; President, Family Planning Association of India, Nagaland Branch and member of its National Council; Vice-President, Indian Council of Social Service, Nagaland Branch; Member, Governing Body, Nagaland Peace Centre and North-East India Council of Social Science Research, Shillong; Member, College Developmental Council, Exam Committee, School Board of Physical Sciences and Board of Undergraduate Studies (Chemistry), NEHU Shillong; Chairman, Board of Hindi Studies and Member, Board of Studies for Science for Rural Development, Gandhigram Rural University (Tamil Nadu); etc.

He is author/editor of about 130 books and more than 100 papers and radio talks in Hindi and English. He contributed papers in a large number of seminars, books and journals, edited. *The Thinker*, quarterly journal for 12 years and Nagaland Special number of *Journal of Social Research*, Ranchi as a guest editor.

He received Ganga Sharan Singh award for the distinguished work in the field of Hindi propagation.

His latest publications include *Tension and Conflict in North-East India*, *Modernization in Naga Society*, and *Folk-Lore & Folk Lore Motifs*.

SMALL STATES SYNDROME IN INDIA

B.B. KUMAR

CONCEPT PUBLISHING COMPANY, NEW DELHI-110059

ISBN 81-7022-691-0

First Published 1998

Published and Printed by
Ashok Kumar Mittal
Concept Publishing Company
A/15-16, Commercial Block, Mohan Garden
NEW DELHI-110059 (India)

Phones : 5504042, 5554042
Fax : 091-11-5558898

In memory of
a few weeks with
Suraj Narayan Singh,
Basawan Singh,
Lakhan Lal Kapoor,
Yuvaraj
and other Friends
in Hazaribagh Central Jail
in December 1963

PREFACE

THE territorial re-organization of British Indian provinces preceded the re-organization of states in free India. The sole purpose of the Britishers in the territorial re-organization and the formation of new provinces was the advancement of the imperial interests and the efficient administration. Development and welfare did not form the agenda of the Britishers. Due weightage was always given to the policy of 'Divide and Rule' in deciding such matters.

The substantial portion of India during the pre-independence days was ruled by the Indian princes. The problem of integration of the Princely states was ably handled by Sardar Patel after the freedom of India. The British also created religious, ethnic and regional divide. The religious divide and the policy of Muslim League resulted into the partition of the country. The regional divide was subdued due to strong nationalism created by the freedom struggle. The caste tribe divide and the resultant problem was tackled by the national leaders. The tribal areas were given autonomy under the fifth and sixth Schedules of the Indian Constitution.

The demands for linguistic states was made very soon. India was linguistically re-organized in 1956. The unrest in Naga Hills district of Assam resulted into the formation of Nagaland. The demands of mini tribal states were repeatedly made. This resulted into the formation of many small states in the country. Many areas were given autonomy, such as in Darjeeling Hills of West Bengal, Jharkhand in Bihar, Bodoland in Assam and Ladakh in Jammu & Kashmir. This has not eased the situation. The demands for autonomy and for many more states continues. The book tells the tale of re-organization of States in India and that of the new state demands. It discusses the problems, retrospects and prospects, myths and realities of the mini states' demands.

I hope the readers would like the book inspite of its shortcomings.

I have intimately seen the functioning of the small states in North-East India. I was immensely benefited from the discussions I had with my tribal and non-tribal friends about their functioning. The dreams and aspirations of the people, their frustrations due to non-delivery of the desired good to the people, etc. continued to be the topics of our discussions. I vividly remembered many remarks of many of my friends. Those remarks helped me in getting a feel of the situation during writing of the book. I gratefully remember my friends of the North-East at this hour.

I thank my son, Ajit Pragya for his help during the preparation of the manuscript. He helped me by preparing some maps. I thank my publisher, Shri Ashok Kumar Mittal of Concept Publishing Company, New Delhi for readily agreeing to undertake the publication of the book.

B.B. KUMAR

CONTENTS

Preface 7
List of Maps 11

THE PROBLEM, MYTHS AND REALITIES

1. Unsettling the Settled 15

THE HISTORICAL PERSPECTIVE

2. The British Indian Provinces and the Native States 29
3. The Merger of Princely States 38
4. The District Level Autonomy Under the Sixth Schedule 47
5. The Linguistic Reorganization of the States 52
6. Nagaland and the Small States Syndrome 59
7. The Experiments of a State within a State: The Case of Meghalaya 66
8. Emergence of other Small States in India 74

OPENING THE NEW CHAPTER

9. The Statehood for Uttarakhand 83

MEETING HALF-WAY

10. The Gorkhaland Imbroglio 91
11. Unending Conflict in Bodoland 101
12. The Jharkhand Movement and the JAAC 113
13. Autonomous Hill Council in Ladakh 122

LOW-KEY STATE DEMANDS

14. Low-key State Demands 129
15. Autonomy Demands in Jammu and Ladakh 141
16. The Demand for the Mithila State 146
17. The Statehood Demand in Karbi-Anglong and North Cachar Hills 150

THE NEW DEMAND

18. And Now Seemanchal 157

ANNEXURES

1. Constitutional Provision for the Formation of New States and Alteration of Boundaries 163
2. The Area of the States and the Union Territories of India 165
3. Population of the Indian States and Union Territories According to 1991 Census 166
4. Subjects and the Departments under the Jurisdiction of Bodoland Autonomous Council 167
5. Uttarakhand—Area and the Population of the Proposed State 169
6. Area and Population of the Jharkhand Region 170
7. Area and Population of Telangana Region 171
8. Vidarbha Region of Maharashtra 172
9. Mithilanchal—The Area and the Population Claimed by the Protagonists 173
10. Autonomy Demand within the State of Jammu & Kashmir 174
11. Regions of Madhya Pradesh Demanding Statehood 175
12. State Autonomy Demands in Assam 176

Bibliography 177

Index 180

LIST OF MAPS

1.1	States, Union Territories and Capitals	16
7.1.	Meghalaya	67
9.1.	Uttarakhand Region, U.P.	84
10.1.	Gorkhaland	91
11.1.	Bodoland	101
12.1.	Jharkhand Autonomous Area	114
12.2.	Proposed Jharkhand Area	115
13.1.	Ladakh Region, Jammu & Kashmir	123
14.1.	Chhattisgarh, Madhya Pradesh	130
14.2.	Bundelkhand Region, Uttar Pradesh	132
14.3.	Bundelkhand Region, Madhya Pradesh	134
14.4.	Telangana Region, Andhra Pradesh	135
14.5.	Vidarbha Region, Maharashtra	137
14.6.	Cachar, Assam	139
15.1.	Jammu Region, Jammu & Kashmir	142
16.1.	Mithilanchal Demand	147
17.1.	Autonomous State Demand Karbi-Anglong and North Cachar Hills, Assam	151

THE PROBLEM, MYTHS AND REALITIES

1

UNSETTLING THE SETTLED

THE Prime Minister, Shri H.D. Deve Gowda's announcement from the ramparts of the Red Fort on this year's Independence day* about the creation of 'Uttarakhand' has brought the issue of reorganization of States in our country to unprecedented focus. The announcement was made in usual solo style of Mr. Deve Gowda without consulting the cabinet or the Steering Committee of the United Front.[1] It has simultaneously generated optimism, scepticism, heat and genuine concern among the people of this country.

The individuals, parties, and the organizations in the fore-fronts of the new States' demands are getting ready for the struggle. The atmosphere is warming up. Rejected politicians are hopeful and are busy in working out new strategies. The newspapers are full of the reports about the formation and re-activation of the 'Sangharsh Samities', new permutations and combinations of the political parties and the organizations; formation of coordination committees, etc. for fighting for the purpose. The emotions are aroused. Threats and warnings are issued. The reasoning and the rationality has taken the back seat.

The age of the 'Thinker Politicians' is over. We are troubled to think of the present day pigmies in the shadow of the giant thinker politicians, like, Gandhiji, Tilak, Gokhale, Ranade, Dada Bhai Naoroji, Bipin Chandra Pal, Lala Lajpat Rai, Nehru, Netaji, Rajaji, Sardar Patel, Rajendra Prasad, Lohia, Jai Prakash Narayan, and so on. The think-tank role of the academicians, researchers, philosophers and thinkers have been hijacked by the politicians, journalists, bureaucrats, and film-stars. At this juncture, ironically, the politicians, the capitalists and the privilege-seeking elite of the society have developed vested interest in keeping the society and the country divided. A divided society, either does not question, or raises very faint voice against the wrong acts, policies,

* On August 15, 1996

A Sketch Map

MAP 1.1 : States, Union Territories and Capitals

decisions and mis-deeds of its political masters. The Prime Minister could make such a vital announcement with such an ease at the questionable time, when U.P. elections were just to be held, because he was sure of the weak questioning power of the nation on such a vital issue.

The demands for Jharkhand, Gorkhaland, Bodoland and Ladakh were agitating the minds of the people for some time. The States went half-way to meet their autonomy demands and they were given 'Autonomous Council' within the framework of the existing States. The leaders of the above-mentioned areas were encouraged to ask for full-fledged States after the announcement of Uttarakhand. Echos of the dead demands for the States were started being heard again. Thus, the announcement unsettled many settled issues.

States Demands: Retrospects and the Prospects

There were three kinds of the administrative arrangements during the British Raj in this country. Annexation of territories and consolidation of the empire formed the core of British policy of India before 1857 Sepoy Mutiny. They followed the policy of non-interference in the internal affairs of the native rulers later on. Thus, three kinds of administrative systems emerging were the following:

(i) The areas under direct control of the British Indian Government; the Governor's, the Lt. Governor's, and the Chief-Commissioner's provinces came under this category;

(ii) The areas under indirect control and administration; the Princely States under overall British Indian paramountcy came under the second category; and

(iii) Certain areas of British India under the controls of the Governors as the agents of the Governor-General. The areas excluded from the proposed reforms had excluded and partially excluded areas and had either no administration or only a scanty administration.

The post-reforms British colonial policy in India was aimed at weakening the Indian solidarity and the national movement. The British successfully planted the communal divide in the mainstream politics which ultimately resulted into partition of the country into India and Pakistan. The shift in the British policy of Subordinate Isolation to Subordinate Union saw further change during post-reforms period. The

Chamber of Princes was formed to unite the native rulers together. The Butler Committee recommendations aimed at their isolation from the mainstream Indian integration. The pronouncement of the lapse of British Paramountcy at the dawn of independence was aimed at keeping India bulkanized. It needed a man like Sardar Patel to solve the monsterous problem created by the British at that time. The ugly designs of the British colonial functionaries; Robert Neil Reid, Andrew Clow, Hutton, Mills, Sir Reginald Coupland, etc. could not succeed. The Coupland Plan to carve out a Crown Colony by combining the hills of India and Burma and thereby separating the excluded and partially excluded areas from India remained a dream only. However, whatever the Britishers did have tremendous unsettling effect and needed utmost devotion, imagination and efforts to settle it.

The unsettling acts of the British Colonial masters in case of the British Indian provinces and the Princely States was settled by Sardar Patel. The colonial plans on the North-Eastern fringe could not succeed due to hasty retreat of the British from the Indian scene. The Sixth Schedule of the Constitution has the provision for the district level autonomy. It settled the problem in the North-East to a great extent. Sardar Patel, Dr. B.R. Ambedkar and Gopi Nath Bordoloi gave constitutional and administrative answers to the problems. They settled the problems in their own way. The hold of the ethnic, regional and linguistic parochial theories of the colonial masters was undermined in the post-independence period. It needed academic and emotional answers and the country failed to respond. The mishandling of the Naga problem further compounded the problem. The insurgency, a low intensity war like situation, prevails in the pockets of the region. Any community, irrespective of the size of population and the area inhabited, demands a State. The logic of gun and not that of the norms, is heard and respected. The wrong signal that 'violence pays' has many takers and the number of such people is steadily increasing.

The colonial Government sponsored studies on the castes, tribes, languages, religion, etc. of India with the aim of depicting India as a confused and divided entity. This was done as a part of the well-laid strategy prepared after 1857 Sepoy Mutiny. The micro studies on castes, tribes, etc. depicted India as a heterogeneous and confused conglomeration of different races, castes, tribes, languages, dialects, regions, religions and sects. They successfully projected the empire as the liberator, the deliverer of good, unifier of India and the best guarantee for safeguarding the interests of the fringe areas, the tribals and the untouchables.[2]

The above-mentioned studies conducted as per the policy framed by Alfred Lyall, an important functionary in the colonial Administration were not followed by macro studies on Indian society by the Indian scholars.[3]

The hold of colonial scholarship is very strong on Indian scholars and elites. The anthropology, linguistics, history, indology, etc. have failed to get rid of the biases of the colonial days. This is why, our studies are overburdened with the emphasis on so called conflict between the core (mainstream) and the fringe, imaginary dangers on ethnic identity, the conflict situation between the Aryans and non-Aryans, exploiters *vs.* exploited, caste *vs.* tribe, etc. The North-Eastern studies are more obsessed in this matter.

The linkage of ethnic identity and the demand for tribal states had the unsettling effect of the worst kind. This has led to forced social, cultural and religious distancing in India. The linguistic parochialism is found to be advantageous in the same way. The social, ethnic and linguistic parochials of the worst kind have become the champions of new State demands throughout India.

The lack of accountability on the part of people running the states have become counter-productive. The State funds are often diverted and misused by the politicians and their retainers. There are scams, overdrawals, LoCs, etc. Of late, of course, the element of fear has been introduced due to 'Judicial Activism'. Nevertheless, politics continues to be the best profession for the unscrupulous persons seeking name, fame and unlimited power and money. More States bring more opportunities, specially for the second and third ranking and rejected politicians. Thus, the demands for more states have become lucrative for many.

The poverty and the flow of funds are linked up. The lack of accountability leads to failure of development schemes and poverty alleviation programmes of the Governments. It also makes money making easier. Thus considerable section of the political elite develop vested interest in perpetuation of poverty.

More States bring more jobs for the educated youth and lot of opportunities for career advancement. This is why the army of unemployed educated persons join the political leaders in this endeavour. The followers of the politicians also need jobs and other gratifications. This leads to over-employment and corruption. This is precisely, why the most of the funds of many small states is spent on the payment of the salary and perks of its employees. The poverty in the most favoured

States is perpetuated; sustainable development continues to remain a far cry, and a very wide gap has emerged between the rich and poor of many small ethnic States of the country within a very short time.

The Small States Demands: Myths and the Realities

The myth is that Sates are always demanding for development, but the development never shows its face to the last man. The fate of the common man of some of the smallest States of the country remains deplorable inspite of the fact that such States have the highest per capita spending on development. The protagonists of the small States spend more and develop less. They are afraid of taking suitable steps to mobilise funds for development. This charge was also labelled against the Autonomous District Councils. The performance of the small States, and that of the Autonomous Area Councils and the District Councils should be studied to evolve suitable policy framework for further reorganization of States in this country.

The talk of dominance, hegemony and exploitation by a section of the State by other is yet the other myth. The common man of Bodo and non-Bodo origin is equally subjected to deprivation. There is exploitation of the common man of Bodo and non-Bodo origin in Assam and that of the Jharkhand and North Bihar origin in Bihar. Thus, such expressions, like 'Assamese hegemony over Bodos' and 'exploitation of Jharkhand by North Bihar' is a hoax. The reality is otherwise. Bihar continues to be the most exploited State in the country and the so called 'exploitation of Jharkhand by North Bihar' is a journalistic bluff. It is unfortunate that the White and Red colonial theoreticians are equally obsessed with the exploitation/hegemonistic theories.

We often read and hear about the problem of identity crisis in this country and the need of protecting the identity of certain vocal groups. The fact that the Indian society is averse to identity obliteration and tends to preserve the identity of numerous castes and tribes by the practice of endogamy is ignored. Moreover, is it necessary to create overemploying State machineries with the army of 'Siters and Eaters' for identity preservation. We need to ponder over the following facts in this connection:

(i) The linguistic States were not sincere to develop the State languages. Similarly, adequate steps were not taken by the 'Ethnic States' to develop the tribal languages. The States asking for the protection of their customary laws and usages have decimally performed in the field of codification of their customary laws and failed to provide justice to the people according to their customs and usages through Tribal Courts. Of course, there are G.B.'s and D.B.'s Courts in certain states, but that is not enough.

(ii) Deliberate and forced social and cultural distancing from the people of the neighbourhood by a section of Indian population is going on the name of identity preservation. The same people blindly follow the foreign culture, insist on adopting foreign language and script and go Western. Hating Assamese-Bengali script and struggling for the Roman script has become a profitable game in Assam and Tripura. It is difficult to understand how there is danger for the identity of certain groups from an Indian script and not from a foreign one? It needs to be mentioned that the script was used for centuries by the tribals and non-tribals alike. The Assamese and Bengali culture and language have taken the present shape due to joint endeavour of all the communities of the areas irrespective of whether they are tribals or non-tribals. If they face any danger, it is from the Western culture and languages.

However, the needs of politics dictate otherwise. The myths are created to meet the needs of politics. It is not necessary that they conform to the realities. It is ironical that the groups which talk against the Assamese/Bengali script in the North-East show keen favours towards Westernization and want the Roman script for the tribal languages of Assam and Tripura. The policy of Social and Cultural distancing is practised to claim separate ethnic identity and separate sub-nationality in North-East India. Autonomy is claimed on the basis of forced or real ethnic identity. The autonomy brings power without responsibility and a lot of loaves without much labour. The claim of autonomy is again strengthened on real or assumed grievances of exploitation, hegemony, neglect, and underdevelopment. It is said that the very leaders, who talk against hegemony and underdevelopment forget their utterances very soon. It is not difficult to find hegemony of dominant groups in smaller States. Sub-regional imbalance is more marked in their case.

The forced social and cultural distancing has reversed the process of emotional integration in Indian society and yet it has become a paying venture. It has also given birth to aggressive minoritism in certain pockets of the country.

Aggressive Minoritism

The formation of linguistic States created linguistic minorities, practically, in every part of the country. This created majority-phobia in many States and aggressive majoritism in many small pockets of the country. It has worked to disturb the pluri-social formations and pluri-social ethos of Indian society. The same phenomenon was repeated in Ethnic States. A large percentage of population suffered likewise, in the new set-up. Aggressive minoritism, however, is a new phenomenon in many respects.

Much of our scholarship, and specially, the journalistic scholarship (if the phrase is correct) is notional in nature. One such notion on which much of the populist and journalistic writings go on is that 'small is aggrieved'. The aggressive, violent and the exclusive postures of many communities are overlooked and justified due to such notions.

The tribals constitute less than 1/3rd population of the Jharkhand area and yet the post of the chairman of the Jharkhand Area Autonomous Council goes to a tribal. The Bodos constitute a hopeless minority in the territories of the Bodoland and they are given powers to control the Bodoland Autonomous Council's affairs. Why? The answer of the question cannot be given in the democratic framework of a civilised society. The Koch-Rajbansis are one of the oldest settlers of Assam. They have more population in the Bodoland area than that of the Bodos. They suffer discrimination and are not given equal political power in the Bodoland Autonomous Council. Why? Because they are not aggressive and have not taken stand of deliberate social and cultural distancing. The Koch-Rajbansis claim to be Kshatriya and a due place in Hindu caste framework. They are trying to gain Scheduled Caste status due to the obvious gains. What their real social status cannot give them, they may get it by the aggressive stand on moving away socially and culturally.

The Santal tribals were settled in Assam by the Britishers. They worked in the tea gardens there and lived harmoniously. A large number of Santals were killed by the Bodos last year. Was it an attempt to scare away non-Bodos from that area? The Bodos want contiguous villages under the Bodoland area with less than 50 per cent Bodo population or no Bodo population at all. Are those unfortunate persons also going to face the fate of the Santals? The Indian State should learn to think in terms of the people of the area and not in terms of the interest of a vocal aggressive groups. The State shall become unmanageable if every group starts speaking through the gun. We should aim at integration and the interests of non-aggressive groups should never be ignored.

Autonomous Area Council Experiments

The formation of Darjeeling Gorkha Hill Council in West Bengal, Bodoland Autonomous Council in Assam, Jharkhand Area Autonomous Council in Bihar and Ladakh Leh Hill Council in Ladakh region of Jammu & Kashmir were the steps taken in right direction. The autonomous Councils have failed to satisfy the people of the regions except that of Leh. Some of the reasons of the same are given below:

(i) Insincerities of the State Governments in the implementation of the accords have created the crisis of confidence. The departments to be run by the Councils are yet to be handed over in some cases. The elections of some of the Councils are yet to be held and the interim Councils are allowed to run the affairs of the Councils.

(ii) There was delay in giving adequate financial and administrative powers to the Councils.

(iii) The cases of lack of co-ordination between the State Governments and the Councils were reported.

(iv) The Igo-complexes of the persons running the States and the Councils came in the way of the smooth implementation of the policies and programmes of the Councils and created doubts about the success of the autonomy experiment.

(v) The cases of financial indiscipline and non-performing work ethos had the demoralising effect.

(vi) Darjeeling Gorkha Hill Council, even, failed to conduct Panchayat elections inspite of repeated request by the West Bengal Government.

(vii) Some politicians involved in running the Councils do not want its success. They wanted Councils as the stepping stones for full-fledged Statehood.

It should be our endeavour to see that the Autonomous Area Councils succeed in achieving the desired level of developmental goals. The success of the experiment shall help in curbing the mad race of State demands to a large extent.

Need of Rational Parameters

The Government has formed economically non-viable small States with very small area and population. The logic and rationality parameters ceased to guide the Government of India in meeting the demands for such States. There are many States run by the over-dose of funds from the Consolidated Fund of India. Such States are not raising the local resources sincerely. They hardly raise 10 to 30 per cent revenue for running the States from the local resources. This tempts many ethnic groups to claim Statehood. The myths mentioned above come handy in support of their separatist claims. The papers in journals and newspapers with usual journalistic oversimplifications justify any claim; glamourise violent movements, bundhs, blockades and the disruptive agitations. Governments ignores even the genuine demands till it remains peaceful, allows things to take bad shape and acts only when the things take bad turn. It even concedes unjust demands when forced to act by appropriate dose of violence. It has failed to send proper signal that 'violent does not pay'.

Heavy administrative machinery proves to be counter-productive. The overemployment leads to unproductive non-revenue generating expenditure. This makes the sustainable development impossible.

The small States of North-East India come under this category. Such States have failed to develop themselves inspite of most favourable per capita plan and non-plan grants. More than 80 per cent of the budget is eaten up by the salary and perks of the employees in many States. The resources do not percolate to the poorest. The gap between the rich and poor has widened. The developmental imbalance between the regions of the smaller States have shockingly increased. Some States have developed vested interest in backwardness.

The Nagaland had only one officer of Deputy Commissioner's rank in pre-independence period. The number of officers in the rank of Commissioner may not be less than a score today. The area had five seats in the Assam Legislative Assembly. Now it has 60-member State Assembly and more than half of the MLAs are ministers. The region had about 120 MLAs in the Assam Legislative Assembly and about a dozen ministers after independence. To-day, the North-Eastern region with about 3 per cent population of the country has over 450 MLAs and about 200 ministers. The expenditure on the salary and perks is very high.

The region receives developmental support from North-Eastern Council. The Prime Minister H.D. Deve Gowda has just announced a 61 billion rupees packages for the region.[4] The region has four Central Universities, an IIT and a Regional Institute of Science and Technology. The input is not lacking, but the development continues to elude.

We should take lessons from the functioning of the smaller States before deciding on further reorganization of the country. The utter ad-hocism in this matter is going to be counter-productive. The backward regions of the backward States have suffered for decades. Their development cannot wait.

Some of the points given below need serious consideration to avoid further complication in this matter:

(i) Any future reorganization of the country should be based on rational parameters.
(ii) A Commission should be set up for the purpose.
(iii) Ad-hocism of any kind should not be allowed in this matter. The formation of any new State should be stopped in future unless, its economic viability, effect on the neighbouring regions, and on regional development, its impact on other similar demands, etc. are thoroughly studied.
(iv) The constitutional amendment should be done to limit the expenditure on salary and perks of the State Government employee, size of the ministry, etc.
(v) The economically non-viable States should be merged together.
(vi) The system of accountability should be developed. The Constitution should be suitably amended to hold the ministers and secretaries responsible for the developmental and other lapses.

The Need of Responsible Political Culture and Social Activism

The present day Political Culture of the Country is responsible for much of the malady. The Political parties take ad-hoc stand on populist considerations and do not have long term policy and programme for the reorganization of the States. They ignore the interest of non-organized and pacific section of the people. The Vote-bank considerations weigh heavily in the minds of the political leaders and there is a feeling that Bangladeshi infiltrators are more secure than many Indians. The general people suffer due to soft State syndrome and militancy. There is need of social activism to force the political elite to behave. The rational distribution of resources among the States is not done by the Centre and many States continue to suffer.

REFERENCES

1. Rajeshwar, T.V., "Now Reap the Whirlwind", *The Hindustan Times*, September 6, 1996.
2. Kumar, B.B., *North-East India : Need for a Fresh Look, The Administrator*, Vol. XXXIX, No. 4, October-December, 1994, p. 11. Also, in *North-East and the Indian State : Paradoxes of a Periphery*, Vikash Publishing House Pvt. Ltd., New Delhi, pp. 19-20.
3. *Ibid.*
4. *The Times of India*, October 28, 1996.

THE HISTORICAL PERSPECTIVE

2

THE BRITISH INDIAN PROVINCES AND THE NATIVE STATES

THE Britishers came to India as traders. The East India Company was a trading company. Initially, the Company started outposts in Calcutta, Bombay (now, Mumbai) and Madras (now, Chennai). They started factories in India after that. In Bengal, the first factory was started in Hugli in 1651 under permission from Sultan Shuja, the then Subehdar of Bengal and the second son of emperor Shahjehan.[1] Mr. Boughton was an employee of the Company. He cured a royal lady and Sultan Shuja was so happy with the act that he granted the Company the privileges of free trade throughout Bengal, Bihar and Orissa for a nominal lump sum payment of Rs. 3000.00 only in the same year. The English factories sprang up soon after in Kassimbazar, Patna and other places.[2]

The Britishers were quick to learn the weaknesses of the Indian rulers. They started playing politics and became so important that they were able to play the supreme role in the affairs of Bengal very soon. The battle of Plassey practically sealed the fate of the Nawabs of Bengal and the East India Company virtually became the ruler of the area after the grant of Diwani of Bengal and Bihar.

The British empire building started around the three nuclei of Calcutta, Bombay and Madras. The acquired territories of east, west and south India were gradually added to the Presidencies of Bengal, Bombay and Madras. This resulted into the formation of three original British Indian provinces. Acquisition of new territories continued, leading to the formation of more and more British Indian provinces. The areas in the central part of the country formed the Central Provinces (CP). The Britishers merged the territories of Agra and Oudh to form the United Provinces of Agra and Oudh. The British acquired Berar and Jhansi in 1853 and Oudh in 1856. The territories were acquired by war. Some territories, such as Jhansi were acquired by the application of the doctrine of lapse. The name of the United Provinces of Agra and Oudh was shortened to the United Province in 1835 and changed to Uttar Pradesh in 1951.

The Sind was annexed in 1943 and merged with Bombay Presidency. The territories of Punjab and North-West Frontier Province were mostly annexed after the conclusion of Anglo-Sikh wars and the Afghan wars. The British formed bigger States during the first phase of the empire building. The second phase of the formation of the British Indian provinces was initiated by the bifurcation of bigger states into smaller ones. The Assam was the first State of its kind.

The sole purpose of the Britishers in the territorial reorganization and the formation of new States was the advancement of the imperial interest and the efficient administration. Development and welfare did not form the agenda of the British State. Due weightage was always given to the furtherance of the policy of 'Divide and Rule'. The British India had three kinds of provinces, namely, the Governor's Provinces, the Lt. Governor's Provinces and the Chief Commissioner's Provinces. The Assam was carved out of the Presidency of Bengal in 1874 as a 'Chief Commissioner's Province'. It was merged with the newly created province of 'East Bengal' in 1905 after the partition of Bengal to form the province of 'East Bengal and Assam'. The status of Assam was restored after the annulment of the partition of Bengal in 1911. The life of the new State was only six years.

The Bengal Presidency was again bifurcated in the year 1912. A new State of Bihar and Orissa was carved out of the same in that year. The entire secretariat of the province of 'East Bengal and Assam' shifted from Dhaka to Patna as the Secretariat of Bihar and Orissa.

The initiative for the separation of the province of 'Bihar and Orissa' from Bengal was taken by Sachchidanand Sinha. He managed the appointment of Sir Ali Imam as a Law Member in the Viceroy's Executive Council. Ali Imam influenced Lord Hardinge for the creation of the new State. Lord Hardinge approved the scheme of separation of Bihar and Orissa from Bengal and wrote to Lord Crew, the Secretary of State for the same. He wrote, "the Biharis are a sturdy loyal people and it is a matter of common knowledge that although they have long cherished separation from asking for it because they did not wish to join the Bengalees in opposition to the Government. There has moreover, been a marked awakening in Bihar in recent years and a strong belief has grown up among Biharis that Bihar will never develop until it is dissociated from Bengal. That belief will, unless a remedy is found, give rise to agitation in near future, and the present is an admirable opportunity to carry out our own initiative a thoroughly sound and much desired change."[3]

The proposal was approved by the Secretary of State and the King Emperor George Vs announced the formation of the new province in Delhi Durbar. The Province was to function under a Lieutenant-Governor in Council. The notification for the creation of new province was issued on 23.3.1912 and it started functioning with effect from April 1, 1912.

The States of Orissa and Sind were born in 1937 and Burma was separated from India in the same year. Orissa was carved out from the province of Bihar and Orissa and the Muslim majority province of Sind from the Bombay Presidency. No new province was born in the British India after 1937. The British India had the following Provinces at the time of independence.

1. Assam
2. Bengal
3. Bihar
4. Bombay
5. Central Provinces or C.P.
6. Madras
7. North-West Frontier Province
8. Orissa
9. Punjab
10. Sind
11. United Provinces or U.P.

India was partitioned in 1947 into India and Pakistan. The Hindu majority provinces of Assam, Bihar, Orissa, Bombay, Madras, United Provinces and the Central Provinces remained with India and the Muslim majority provinces of Baluchistan, Sind and North-West Frontier Province joined Pakistan. The Punjab and Bengal were partitioned into two parts. East Punjab and West Bengal remained with India and West Punjab and East Bengal joined Pakistan.

The Governor's and Chief-Commissioner's provinces had uniform system of administration. They were under cent per cent control of the Britishers. That was not the case with the States controlled by the native rulers. Their administration was mostly autocratic. The dividing line between the State revenue and the personal finances of the rulers was mostly absent. The British control of the Princely States was mainly aimed at the advancement of their imperial and commercial interests. The welfare of the people of the States did not bother them. This is the reason that most of the territories under the control of the Princely rulers, with few exceptions, continued to be very backward.

India during the British period was not uniformly controlled and various regions may be categorised as given below:

(i) Areas under effective British control,
(ii) Partially administered areas,
(iii) Unadministered areas, and
(iv) The areas controlled by the native princes.

I have already dealt with the first category above. The next two categories were mostly in the border areas of the North-East. The fourth category under the Princely State had varied degrees of inner control. The British control in these areas was mostly through the princes who functioned under the British Paramountcy. Initially, the British treated them on equal terms, but gradually the status of the native princes was lowered. The following observation of B.B. Kumar about the rulers of North-East India equally applies to the large number of cases:

> "The British were not aware of the strengths and weaknesses of the rulers of this region and were very cautious in their dealings with them. Their cautious approach gradually gave way to unusual firmness. The Kings and Chiefs who were initially treated on equal footings, were gradually reduced to the status of Sanad and Kabuliat holders. British paramountcy gradually eclipsed the sovereignty of the kings. This gradually happened as British established their stronghold on other parts of the country and could know the inner weaknesses of the society, the ruling elite and the polity of the region."[4]

The status of the petty kings was so low that they were even kept under the general control and authority of the Deputy Commissioner of a district. The following sentence from Article 1 of the 'Engagement with Rajah of Mahram, 1864' makes my point clear.

> "I consider myself under the general control and the authority of the Deputy Commissioner in the Cossiah and Jynteah Hills, or such other officer as may be, from time to time, appointed by the Government. . . ."[5]

The position of the medium sized States was only slightly better. The contents of the Sanad issued to Raja Chura Chand Singh, Maharaja of Manipur amply illustrate the matter. The terms of Sanad and grant of titles clearly indicate that the status of Manipur was not more than that of the vassal in a feudal state.[6] The articles of Sanad are worth noting and are given below:

1. The Governor-General-in-Council has been pleased to select you, Chura Chand, son of Choubi Yaima to be the Chief of the Manipur State and you are hereby granted the title of Raja of Manipur and a salute of eleven guns.
2. The chiefship of the Manipur State and the title and salute will be hereditary in your family and will descend in the direct line by primogeniture provided that in each case the succession is approved by the Government of India.
3. The annual tribute will be paid by you and your successors to the British Government.
4. Further, you are informed that permanence of the grant conveyed by the Sanad will depend on the ready fulfilment by you and your successors of orders given by the British Government with regard to the administration of your territory, the control of the hill tribes dependent upon Manipur, the composition of armed forces of the State and any other matter in which the British Government may be pleased to interfere. Be assured that so long as your house is loyal to the Crown and faithful to the conditions of this Sanad, you and your successors will enjoy the favour and protection of the British Government.[7]

The Sanad demanded loyalty and subordination. The interference by British Government increased day by day in Manipur affairs due to in-built mechanism developed on the basis of the terms of the above-mentioned Sanad. The powers of the Raja were gradually reduced. The usual practice of the Manipur Darbar that the Raja presided over the meetings of Darbar was changed. The Vice-President appointed by the British started presiding over the meetings of the Darbar and then the President was appointed by the British. The charge of the Superintendent of Police and that of the State armed forces was taken over by the British officers from the hands of the Princes. Raja did not have powers to appoint the Chief-Judge, select his Prime Minister, to remove members of his Darbar, to determine the civil-list, to frame State administration rules, etc.[8] The examples may be multiplied. The same was the fate of most of other Rajas of the country.

The British had power without responsibility in the affairs of the native States of India.

The Changing British Policy Towards the Indian States

Sir William Lee-Warner in his book entitled *The Native States of India* have mentioned about the three phases of the British policy towards the Indian States during pre-reform period.[9] The three phases are summed up below :

(i) The Ring Fence Policy followed during the earlier period of the rule of East India Company during 1757-1813 emphasised the policy of non-interference in the internal matters of the Indian States. The East India Company was one among many powerful centres of power and the policy was based on the realization of its inherent weaknesses. However, the Company did fight many wars during that period inspite of the avowed policy of non-intervention in the affairs of Indian States declared in Pitt's India Act of 1784. Lee-Warner has summed up the policy of the period in the following words:

> "The British endeavoured as far as possible to live within a Ring-Fence, and beyond that they avoided intercourse with the chiefs."[10]

(ii) The Policy of Subordinate Isolation was followed during 1813-1857. The Indian States were made to enter into subsidiary alliances with the British and to accept British as the paramount power. The British were made the protectors and arbitrators and were paid in cash or given territory for the same by the States. The non-British/non-European employees were turned out by the native rulers under the new arrangement. Lord Hastings brought 310 States of Central India, Kathiawar and Rajputana under the system. Lord Dalhousie did not follow his policy and annexed many States by war and the doctrine of lapse.

(iii) *Policy of Subordinate Union* : The Policy of Subordinate Isolation was abandoned after the Sepoy Mutiny of 1857 and the new policy was followed afterwards between 1857-1919.

The policy of annexation and subsidiary alliance created a lot of discontent in India and were considered to be the main reasons of the mutiny. This is why, the policy of subordinate Isolation and Dalhousie's policy of annexation were abandoned after the mutiny. The Queen's proclamation of 1858 declared that the British would not annex the territory of any Indian ruler after that date. It said:

> "We hereby announce to the Native Princes of India that all treaties and engagements made with them by or under the authority of the honourable East India Company are by us accepted and will be scrupulously maintained, and we look for the like observance on their part. We, desire no extension of our present territorial possessions. We shall respect the Rights, Dignity and Honour of the Native Princes as our own. The Indian rulers were to be given the right of adoption in case they had no son to succeed them. No State was to be annexed on the ground that the ruler had no son. The Indian States were to be given Sanads and we are told that 160 Sanads were issued to the Indian rulers."[11]

Issuing of Sanads perpetuated the treaties and engagements between the British and the rulers. The territories under the control of the native rulers were brought under a unified Indian Political system.

The new system did not debar the British Government from taking action against an Indian Prince. Lord Canning made the point clear that the Sanads "will not debar the Government of India from stepping in to set right such serious abuses in a native Government as may threaten any part of the country with anarchy or disturbance, nor from assuming temporary charge of a native State when there will be sufficient reason to do so. . . . Neither will this assurance diminish our right to visit a State with the highest penalties, even confiscation, in the event of disloyalty or flagrant breach of engagement."[12]

Thus, we find that Sanads did not ensure any fair deal to the Indian rulers. There was ample scope for meddling into the internal affairs of the States by the British officers and they often misused their powers.

In many cases, as we have seen in case of Manipur, the authority of the ruler was gradually and systematically curtailed. The marginalization of the King's authority was a painful affair for many of them which they silently suffered.

The extension of British Paramountcy over the Indian States had the desirable effect of uniting this vast country. The link was somewhat loose, but nevertheless, most effective. The merger of Princely States after the dawn of independence further strengthened the links and brought uniformity.

Post-reform Developments

The need of joint consultation and discussion by the Indian rulers for the furtherance of their common interests was felt by the authors of the Montagu-Chelmsford Report. The Chamber of Princes was set up on February 8, 1921 by a Royal Proclamation as a result of the same. A passage from the proclamation is given below:

> "My Viceroy will take its counsel freely in matters relating to the territories of the Indian States generally and in matters that affect these territories jointly with British India or with the rest of my empire. It will have no concern with the internal affairs of individual States or their Rulers or with the relations of individual States with my Government, while the existing rights of these States and their freedom of action will in no way be prejudiced or impaired."

The Chamber of Princes had 120 members. 108 States were represented by their individual Rulers. 127 States were represented by 12 members only. About 327 States were not given representation. A few important States refused to join the forum. The Chamber was a deliberative, consultative and advisory body.

The Simon Commission underlined the importance of the Chamber of Princes in the following statement:

> "The establishment of the Chamber of Princes marks an important stage in the development of relations between the Crown and the States, for it involves a definite breach in an earlier policy, according to which it was rather the aim of the Crown to discourage joint action and joint consultation between the Indian States and to treat each State as an isolated unit apart from its neighbours. That principle, indeed, has already been giving place to the idea of conference and co-operation amongst the ruling princes of India, but this latter conception was not embodied in permanent shape until the Chamber of Princes was established. The Chamber has enabled thorough interchange of views to take place on weighty matters concerning

relationship of States with the Crown and concerning other points of contact with British India."

The Chamber of Princes provided opportunity to the Princes for formal and informal meetings between them. The annual meeting was presided by the Viceroy and in his absence by the Chancellor of the Chamber of Princes. The meetings of the Standing Committee of the Chamber were held 2-3 times in a year in Delhi.

The Butler Committee Recommendations

The three member Committee with Sir Hercourt Butler as chairman and Prof. W.S. Holdsworth and S.C. Peel was constituted by the Secretary of State for India on December 16, 1927. The Committee visited 16 Indian States in January 1928. It heard the views of the Princes and their counsel, but not of the people of the territories. The Committee recommended that the Viceroy to be the agent of the Crown in dealing with the States, rather than the Governor-General-in-Council and that the relations between the Crown and the Princes should not be transferred without the consent of the Princes to a new Government in British India responsible to the legislature. The Committee advised to reject the scheme of the creation of a State Council and enunciated the theory of direct relationship between the State and the Crown. Thus, its recommendations, basically, were aimed at distancing of two categories of the Indian Provinces and the Native States. Naturally, the leaders could see through the colonial game and criticised it. Government of India Act, 1935, on the contrary provided for the federal set-up for both.

REFERENCES

1. Grover, B.L. and S. Grover, *A Look at Modern Indian History*, p. 70.
2. *Ibid.*
3. Quoted by N.M.P. Srivastava in "Recreating History", *The Hindustan Times*, Monday Extra (Patna), April 1, 1996.
4. Kumar, B.B. *The Trends of British Annexation of North-East India*, p. 2.
5. *Ibid.*, p. 107.
6. *Ibid.*, p. 32.
7. *Ibid.*
8. *Ibid.*, pp. 33-34.
9. Mahajan, V.D. *India Since 1526*, p. 545.
10. *Ibid.*, quoted.
11. *Ibid.*, quoted on p. 547.
12. *Ibid.*, quoted on p. 547.

3

THE MERGER OF PRINCELY STATES

THE merger of Princely States in the Indian Dominion was the most important phenomenon of the post-independence period. The country had nine Governor's provinces, three Chief Commissioner's provinces (Delhi, Coorg and Ajmer-Merwara) and about 500 Princely States at the time of independence. The transfer of British paramountcy from the British to the Indian State did not take place in the case of the princely States. The Cabinet Mission in its *Memorandum of States' Treaties and Paramountcy* presented to the Chancellor of the Chamber of Princes on May 22, 1946 stated:

> "When a new fully self-governing or independent Government or Governments come into being . . . His Majesty's government will cease to exercise the powers of paramountcy. This means that the rights of the States which flow from their relationship to the Crown will no longer exist and that all the rights surrendered by States to the Paramount power will return to the States. Political arrangements between the States on the one side and the British Crown and the British India on the other hand, will thus be brought to an end. The void will have to be filled either by the States entering into a federal relationship with the successor Government or Governments in British India, or failing this, entering into particular political arrangements with it or them."[1]

The Cabinet Mission recommended thus:

"1. There should be a Union of India, embracing both British India and the States, which should deal with the following subjects : Foreign Affairs, Defence and Communications; and should have the power necessary to raise the finances required for the above subjects.

2. The States should retain all subjects and powers other than those ceded to the Union."[2]

The Cabinet Mission's plan was accepted by the Princely States. The Standing Committee of the Chamber of Princes resolved on January 29, 1947:

"1. The entry of the States into the Union shall be on no other basis than that of negotiation, and the final decision will rest with each State . . . which can only be taken after consideration of the complete picture of the Constitution.
2. All the rights surrendered by the States to the Paramount power will return to the States. The proposed Union of India will, therefore, exercise only such functions in relation to the States in regard to Union Subjects as are assigned or delegated by them to the Union. Every State shall continue to retain its sovereignty and all rights and powers except those that have been expressly delegated by it. There can be no question of any powers being vested or inherent or implied in the Union in respect of the States unless specifically agreed to by them.
3. The Constitution of each State, its territorial integrity and the succession of its reigning dynasty in accordance with the law, customs and usages of the State, shall not be interfered with by the Union or any part thereof."[3]

Needless to say that the rulers of the States were encouraged by the statements of the Cabinet Mission of May 16, 1946, which pronounced:

> "It is quite clear that with the attainment of independence by British India whether inside or outside of the commonwealth, the relationship which has hitherto existed between the Rulers of the States and the British Crown, will no longer be possible. Paramountcy can neither be retained by the British Crown nor transferred to the new Government. . . . At the same time the States are ready and willing to co-operate in the new development of India. The precise form which their co-operation will take must be a matter for negotiations during the building up of the new constitutional structure, and it by no means follows that it will be identical for all the States."[4]

Thus the Cabinet Mission's statements created a most fluid situation at that critical juncture. The All-India Congress Committee and the national leaders did not like the Cabinet Mission's memorandum and the 'lapse of paramountcy'. Dr. Ambedkar found the flawed theory of 'lapse of paramountcy' against the British Constitutional Law and the

International Law as per his statement dated June 15, 1947.[5] The Muslim League's attitude was, however, favourable.

'Indian States Department' was created under the Home Ministry on July 5, 1947 to deal with matters arising between the Central Government and the Indian States. Sardar Patel took charge of the department. Sardar Patel and Lord Mountbatten advised the States to join the Indian Union. Most of the States conceded to their advice and signed the 'Instrument of Accession'. The Instrument of Accession provided that, pending the promulgation of a Constitution by the Constituent Assembly, in which the States would be adequately represented, the Dominion Parliament would legislate for the acceding States in matters relating to Defence, External Affairs, Communications and other ancillary subjects.

The States' affairs were properly handled and most of them signed the merger agreement without much delay and without difficulty. Junagarh, Hyderabad, Jammu & Kashmir and Travancore gave some trouble. The merger of the States followed different patterns depending mostly on the size, geographical location, cultural affinity, etc. of the States concerned. It took the following courses:

1. Very small States were merged with the Governor's provinces. 39 Eastern States with the area of 56,000 sq. miles and the population of 70 lakhs were merged with Orissa and Central Provinces on January 1, 1948. Seventeen Deccan States (and later on Kolhapur) with an area of 10,860 sq. miles and 27 lakhs population merged with Bombay in March, 1948. 289 Gujarat States with 17, 680 sq. miles area and 27 lakhs population joined Bombay presidency in June, 1948. Baroda joined the State in May, 1949. It had 8,236 sq. miles area and 30 lakhs population. Similarly, Khasi Syiemships joined Assam; Rampur, Benaras and Tehri-Garhwal joined United Provinces; Sandur, Pudukotto and Banganapalli were merged with Madras; Kharsawa and Saraikela with Bihar and some very small States with Punjab. Mayurbhanj joined Orissa.

2. Some States were merged together to form Union of States. Some of the States Unions were the following:

(i) United States of Kathiawar (Saurashtra) with 222 States, estates and Taluka, 21,451 sq. miles area and 41 lakhs population was inaugurated on February 15, 1948. Junagarh and some other adjoining States joined it on December 31, 1948.

(ii) United States of Matsya with Bharatpur, Alwar, etc. was inaugurated on March 18, 1948 and the United States of

Rajasthan on March 25, 1948. The United States of Rajasthan included Mewar and nine other small States of Rajputana. Again, the States of Jaipur, Jodhpur, Bikaner and Jaisalmer were included in that Union. Lastly, the United States of Matsya was merged in the same on 15th May, 1948.

(iii) The Union of Himachal Pradesh consisting of 21 States in East Punjab with an area of 10,600 sq. miles and the population of 10 lakhs was inaugurated on 15th April, 1948.

(iv) Thirty-five States of Bundelkhand and Baghelkhand with 24,600 sq. miles area and 36 lakhs population were incorporated into the United State of Vindhya Pradesh on April 4, 1948. It had a responsible ministry, but was made a Centrally administered area on January 1, 1950.

(v) The Madhya Bharat Union with the States of Gwalior, Indore and Malwa with an area of 46,710 sq. miles and the population of 80 lakhs was inaugurated on 28th May, 1948.

(vi) Seven States of East Punjab, such as, Patiala, Kapurthala, Nabha, etc. with an area of 10,999 sq. miles and 35 lakhs population were merged into PEPSU (Patiala and East Punjab States Union). This State was inaugurated on 20th August, 1948.

(vii) Travancore and Cochin were merged together.

3. The single identity of the States, like Mysore, Manipur, Tripura, Cooch-Behar, Bilaspur, Kutch, Hyderabad, Jammu & Kashmir and Bhopal was maintained for some time. Kutch (17,249 sq. miles area, 5 lakhs population) was merged into the Indian Union in May, 1948 as a Chief-Commissioner's province. Karnataka, Manipur, Tripura (15th October, 1949), Bhopal (1st June, 1949), Bilaspur (in Punjab; 12th October, 1948) were merged in the Indian Union with much difficulty. However, the same was not the case with Hyderabad, Junagarh, and Jammu & Kashmir.

Pakistan's Overtures to Princely States

While India tried to secure the merger of States into the Indian Union, Pakistan was also not sitting idle. Princely States of North-West Frontier and other parts of that country were merged with Pakistan. Jinnah offered tempting terms to the Maharajas of Jodhpur and Jaisalmer for the merger of their States into Pakistan.[6] The population of the two States and the Maharajas were Hindus and Jinnah could not succeed in securing the merger of these States into Pakistan. However, the Nawab of Jamnagar, with 85 per cent Hindu population signed the merger document with Pakistan. The State on the southern tip of Saurashtra was about 300 miles away from Karachi. Situation very soon worsened there and the State was merged to India.

Jinnah tried to persuade the Maharaja of Kashmir to join Pakistan. When the persuasion failed, he violated the Stand-still agreement and also sent infiltrators for securing the merger. He accepted the merger of Junagarh and approved the defiant stands of the rulers of Hyderabad and Travancore.

Declaration of Sovereignty

Sir C.P. Ramaswami Aiyar declared on June 11, 1947 that the State of Travancore had decided to become an independent sovereign State. The Nizam of Hyderabad made similar announcement on June 15, 1947.[7] The Nawab of Bhopal who was Chancellor of the Chamber of Princes adopted unfavourable 'sitting on the fence' attitude. His stand was vehemently criticised by the Maharaja of Bikaner, who did not like his policy of 'Wait and see'. The Nawab resign his post and it was taken by the Maharaja of Patiala. The Maharajas of Bikaner and Patiala wanted the participation of Indian States in the Constituent Assembly. Their lead was followed by other princes. The Chancellor, Nawab of Bhopal opposed such move and tried to persuade other princes to follow him. He resigned his post ultimately.[8] He wrote in his letter of resignation:

> "Now that your excellency has indicated to us the policy of His Majesty's Government in regard to the future of the Indian States, and Bhopal State would, as soon as Paramountcy is withdrawn, be assuming an independent status, I consider it desirable that I should tender my resignation of the office of the Chancellor of Princes with effect from to-day. Another reason for my resignation is that the Chamber, as now constituted, formed part of a constitutional machinery which in my opinion, will now become functus officio."[9]

The Nawab wrote another letter to the Viceroy also. He wrote, "the State of Bhopal does not wish to remain associated in any manner whatsoever with the Chamber of Princes or any of its subordinate organizations. It cannot therefore be represented by the Standing Committee of that body and will negotiate direct with the successor Government of British India in regard to its interests, and its future political relationship with Pakistan and Hindustan."[10]

The above-mentioned statements throw enough light on the haziness in the affairs of the Indian State at that moment.

Junagarh

As stated above, the Nawab of Junagarh signed the Instrument of Accession in favour of Pakistan. It has 3,337 sq. miles area and 6,70,719 population (1941 Census). The area of other Kathiawar States was interspersed in between. Jam Saheb of Nawanagar and other rulers of Kathiawar resented the action of the Nawab. They wanted Government of India to take action against the Nawab. There was large scale disturbances and the Hindu refugees were pouring out. The situation became grave. The leaders of Kathiawad established 6 membered provisional Government (*Arzi Hakumat*) on 25.9.1947 and marched from Bombay to Jamnagar. The Government of India took over the State on October 22, 1947 to prevent flare up.

Hyderabad

The Nizam of Hyderabad wanted a dominion status for his State. He issued a *firman* after the announcement of the British Government's plan of transfer of power on 3rd June, 1947 that he would not join the Constituent Assembly of either India or Pakistan and his State would be independent one on August 15, 1947. The Nizam sent a delegation to Lord Mountbatten on July 11, 1947 with Sir Walter Monckton as one of the members. The delegates wanted the restoration of Berar to Hyderabad, grant of dominion status for the State and the Standstill Agreement. A firm 'No' was conveyed to them regarding the first two demands and that no Standstill Agreement would be possible without signing the Instrument of Accession. They threatened to join Pakistan if pressed hard. Nizam wanted two months time for considering the proposals.

Nizam wanted an independent Hyderabad with treaty relations with India about Rail-communications and sharing the forces for the defence of India if allowed to remain neutral in case of Indo-Pakistan war. Such proposals were not entertained by the Government of India. The replacement of the term 'Article of Association' for 'Instrument of Accession' was outright rejected by Patel, as it was certainly to have adverse impact on the rulers who already joined India. The proposal of referendum by Mountbatten was rejected by Nizam. Ultimately, the Standstill Agreement was signed. Mountbatten hoped that Nizam might ultimately sign the Instrument of Accession. The other side wanted breathing time and to get Indian troops out of the boundaries of the Hyderabad State. Patel, however, did not share the optimism of Mountbatten, in this particular case. The Standstill agreement signed on 29th November, 1947 did not generate confidence due to the happenings before and after that date. The Nizam, in his letter dated 18 September, 1947 wanted a treaty of Association short of Accession. The negotiations continued and ultimately the delegate of Hyderabad State left for Hyderabad with an agreed draft on 22.10.1947 for seeking the approval of Nizam. The delegate was to return back to Delhi after four days. However, it did not happen.

A crowd of 25-30 thousand people surrounded the houses of Sir Walter Monchton, Nawab of Chhattari and Sir Sultan Ahmed in the early hours of 26 October, 1947; shouted slogans that the delegates would not go for the negotiation. Kasim Rizwi was the leader of the mob. Nizam informed Lord Mountbatten about the breaking down of the negotiations with India and about initiating negotiations with Pakistan, which he had already initiated. Kasim Rizvi met Patel in Delhi, rejected proposals of merger and plebiscite, and declared sword to be the final arbitrator in case the Government of India insisted on plebiscite. In spite of all these, Mountbatten hoped for the best.

The Nizam started pressing hard for the speedy withdrawal of the Indian troops from the State. The provocative activities of the Razakars of Kasim Rizwi and that of the Majlis Ittehad-ul-Muslimin continued inside the State. The border incidents with Madras, Central Provinces and Bombay threatened the prospects of peace, law and order. Nizam did neither sign the instrument of merger nor introduced the responsible Government in the State. The situation continued to worsen. A final letter was sent to Nizam on 11th September, 1948 by the Government of India stating that they considered themselves free now to take whatever action they thought necessary to restore law and order. Indian troops marched into Hyderabad on September 13, 1948. Armed forces of Hyderabad State surrendered on September 18, 1948. The Police action by the Government of India lasted for about 5 days. The law and order was gradually established. Hyderabad acceded to the Indian Union on January 26, 1950.

The State had an area of 82,000 sq. miles and six crores population. 85 per cent population of the State was Hindu.

Jammu & Kashmir

Jammu & Kashmir with an area of 84,471 sq. miles was ruled by a Hindu Maharaja. The three regions of the State, namely, Kashmir Valley, Jammu and Laddakh have Muslims, Hindus and the Buddhists in majority. The Maharaja wanted his State to remain a sovereign independent State. The State was contiguous to both India and Pakistan.

Pakistan wanted its accession due to Muslims being in the majority. However, neither the Maharaja, nor the people under the leadership of Sheikh Abdullah wanted its merger with Pakistan.

There was no road communication between India and Kashmir prior to the announcement of the Radcliffe Award. The Maharaja proposed to have Standstill Agreement with India and Pakistan. Pakistan signed it, but India was not interested even after restoration of road communication after the Radcliffe Award, Pakistan, inspite of the agreement stopped the road/rail communication and the supply of petrol and essential commodities to the State. It, simultaneously, kept open the channel of dialogue to pursue the ruler to accede to Pakistan. Efforts were made to instigate people to join Pakistan. When the persuasion and threats failed to yield the desired fruits, the Government of Pakistan sent armed raiders to capture the State. Srinagar was threatened. Maharaja appealed for Indian help on 24 October, 1947 which was denied till the State signed the Instrument of Accession.

The Maharaja acceded to the Indian Union on October 26, 1947. His action was fully supported by Sheikh Abdullah and his All Jammu & Kashmir National Conference. The Indian troops were air-lifted to Kashmir on the morning of 27th October, 1947. An interim Emergency Administration headed by Sheikh Abdullah was immediately formed. India took the case of Pakistani aggression to the Security Council on 31st December, 1947 and the cease-fire agreement was signed between India and Pakistan just before the midnight of January 1, 1949.

Categories of the States

India, that is Bharat, was proclaimed to be a Sovereign Democratic Republic and a Union of States on 26th January, 1950. The merger of Princely States was almost complete by that time. The country had following categories of States at that time:

Category A: Assam, Bihar, Bombay, Madhya Pradesh (Central Provinces and Berar), Madras, Orissa, Punjab (East Punjab), the United Provinces (U.P.) and the West Bengal. These States continued to be headed by the Governors as was the case during the British days. They were allowed to have the elected Legislative Assemblies and the Councils of the Ministers.

Category B: The erstwhile Princely States/State Unions included in this category were Hyderabad, Jammu & Kashmir, Madhya Bharat, Mysore, PEPSU (Patiala and East Punjab States Union), Rajasthan, Saurashtra, Travancore-Cochin, and Vindhya Pradesh. The Maharaja of the State functioned as the Raj Pramukh of the State. In Jammu & Kashmir, it was termed Sadar-e-Riyasat. One of the Maharajas acted as the Raj Pramukh in the case of the State Union.

Category C: Included the Chief-Commissioner's provinces of Ajmer, Bhopal, Bilaspur, Coorg, Delhi, Himachal Pradesh, Kutch, Manipur, Tripura and Cooch Behar. This included three pre-existing Chief Commissioner's Provinces, namely, Delhi, Coorg and Ajmer-Merwara.

Category D: The Andaman & Nicobar Islands.

The Process at Work after Independence

The following two processes were initiated at the dawn of independence in India by the national leaders.

(i) *Integration of the country:* All parts of the country were not equally integrated by the Britishers. The national leadership took effective steps to integrate the following in the national mainstream:

 (a) The Princely States were brought under unified constitutional frame-work. The people of these States were no more subjected to the autocratic excesses and the tyranies of their rulers.

 (b) Uniform administration was gradually extended throughout the country. This was not so during the British days when a very large area of the country remained either non-administered or partially administered.

(ii) The entire country was uniformly democratised. This brought a change in the quality of life of the people of the Princely States of this country.

REFERENCES

1. Majumdar, R.C., H.C. Raychaudhuri and Kalikinkar Datta, *An Advanced History of India*, p. 982.
2. *Ibid.*
3. *Ibid.*, pp. 982-83.
4. *Ibid.*, p. 982.
5. *Ibid.*, p. 983.
6. Mahajan, V.D., *India Since 1526*, p. 577.
7. *Ibid.*, p. 562.
8. *Ibid.*
9. *Ibid.*
10. *Ibid.*

4

THE DISTRICT LEVEL AUTONOMY UNDER THE SIXTH SCHEDULE

THE Constituent Assembly of India formed an Advisory Committee on Tribal Areas under the Chairmanship of Sardar Vallabhbhai Patel to consider the problems of Assam and the tribal areas. The Advisory Committee formed a sub-committee under the chairmanship of Gopi Nath Bordoloi. Two members were co-opted by the Bordoloi Committee from each district except from the Frontier Tracts.

Bordoloi Committee

The Bordoloi Committee toured extensively throughout the tribal areas of the country; collected the opinions of the people; considered their demands and formulated the recommendations. The Constituent Assembly, almost entirely accepted the report and the recommendations of the Bordoloi Committee.

The Sixth Schedule

The Bordoloi Committee report and the recommendations were fully discussed in the Constituent Assembly, accepted and incorporated in the form of Fifth and Sixth Schedules in Article 244 of the Constitution. The Fifth Schedule incorporates provisions for the administration and control of the Scheduled Tribes and areas of the States other than Assam. The Sixth Schedule has similar provision for the Scheduled Tribes and areas of Assam.

The constitutional provisions for district level autonomy for the Garo Hills, United Khasi and Jaintiya Hills, the Lushai Hills, the Naga Hills, the North Cachar Hills and the Mikir Hills are incorporated in Part-A of the Sixth Schedule. Similarly, the provisions for the Constitution of the Regional Councils for the Balipara Frontier Tract, Sadiya Frontier

Tract, Tirap Frontier Tract, Abor Area and the Naga Tribal Area of the North-East Frontier Tract were incorporated in Part-B of the Sixth Schedule. These constitutional provisions incorporated in the Sixth Schedule gave greater autonomy to the tribal districts and tracts of North-East India.

The District and the Regional Councils

There is provision for the Constitution, power to make law, administration of Justice in autonomous districts and regions, etc. in the Sixth Schedule of the Constitution. The Schedule was considerably modified by the Act 55 of 1969 and the Act 81 of 1971.

The District and the Regional Councils were given certain legislative, executive and judicial powers under the provisions of the Schedule. These Councils were empowered to make laws with respect to the following:

(i) the allotment, occupation or use, or the setting apart of land—other than reserved forest land,
(ii) the management of forests other than the reserved forests,
(iii) the use of land or water course for agricultural purpose,
(iv) the regulation of the practice of *jhum* or other forms of shifting cultivation,
(v) the matters related to village or town administration, including village or town police and public health and sanitation,
(vi) the establishment of the village or Town Committees or Councils and their powers,
(vii) the appointment or succession of chiefs,
(viii) the inheritance of property,
(ix) social customs, and
(x) marriage.

The Councils are empowered to make regulation for the control of money-lending and trading by non-officials.

The Councils are also empowered to do the following:

(i) to constitute courts for the trial of suits and cases between the parties belonging to the Scheduled Tribes,
(ii) establishment and management of primary schools,
(iii) to determine the language and the manner in which the primary education shall be imparted in the primary schools in the district,

(iv) establishment and management of dispensaries, markets and cattle ponds, and
(v) maintenance of roads and water-ways, etc.

The Governor of Assam was empowered to make rules for the first Constitution of District and Regional Councils in consultation with the existing Tribal Councils or other representative tribal organizations within the autonomous districts or regions. The rules made thus should provide for:

(i) their composition and allotment of seats,
(ii) delimitation of territorial constituencies for election purpose,
(iii) qualification for voting, preparation of electoral rolls,
(iv) the qualification of members,
(v) the terms of office of members,
(vi) matters related to elections/nomination of members,
(vii) the procedure and conduct of business, and
(viii) the appointment of officers and staff, etc.

Special Powers of the Governor

The Governor of Assam was given special powers, as a safeguard, about the District and Regional Councils. He had the powers of suspension, resolution and supersession of the Councils. The assent of the Governor was necessary on the rules, regulations and laws passed by the Councils. He was given the power to appoint the Commission of enquiry into the administration of the Councils.

Continuance and Extension of the Provisions of Sixth Schedule

The Sixth Schedule gave unique status to the tribal areas of North-East. The following provisions gives the Councils special powers:

> "No Act of the State Legislature in respect of tribal affairs shall apply to any autonomous districts unless the District Councils so direct."

On the other hand these areas were given full share in the State Legislature and the State Cabinet.

The District Councils were formed in all the districts of Assam except in the Naga Hills district. The District Councils continued to function in the Garo Hills, United Khasi & Jaintiya Hills and the Lushai Hills (renamed Mizo Hills) districts even after the formation of the State of Meghalaya with former two districts and Mizoram with the last one. Even new District Councils were formed in the two States. The Manipur (Hill Areas) District Councils Act, 1971 was passed to enable Manipur Government to form District Councils in the hill areas of Manipur. The District Councils were also formed in Tripura in 1980s.

More Powers to the District Councils

A meeting of the members of the Executive Committees of the District Councils was held at Shillong on June 16, 1954. The demand for the creation of 'Eastern Hill State' was voiced in the meeting. However, the members of the North Cachar hills District Council and those of the Lushai Hills District Council opposed the demand for a separate State and wanted more autonomy to the District Councils by amending the Sixth Schedule.

The All Party Hill Leaders Conference after its formation on November 2, 1960 demanded a separate State and also the retention and strengthening of the District and Regional Councils. The Nehru Plan promised 'amendment of Sixth Schedule to give more powers to the District and Regional Councils as a part of the autonomy package to the hill leaders of the North-East region. The Pataskar Commission wanted powers to be given to the District Councils.

The Mehta Plan also suggested that maximum autonomy should be given at the district level. More powers were promised to the District Councils under the 'Autonomous State of Meghalaya'.

Drawbacks in the Functioning of the District Councils

As already stated the District Councils were formed to provide maximum autonomy to the hill areas under the frame-work of Assam State. It was an attempt to satisfy the people of the Assam hills that the instrument of the Council was devised. There was no need for the Councils if the hills were to have their separate States. Now the hill people of many districts have their States as well as the costly instrument of the District Councils. The duplicacy should have been avoided. It may be pointed out that most of the funds of the Councils continued to be consumed under salary head, T.A., etc. and very little fund was left for the Development work by them. Moreover, the Councils did not properly use their taxation powers and failed to mobilise resources properly and therefore relied more and more on Government grants. There was resource crunch as the avenues of taxation were not tapped properly, taxation powers were sparingly used and the levied taxes were half-heartedly collected leading to the leakage of revenue.[1]

One of the drawbacks in the functioning of the Councils was the lack of constitutional provision for the coordination of their activities with that of the State governments. Thus, they used to work independently of the State Governments. The Councils did not make full use of their legislative, executive and judicial powers.[2]

In most of the cases, there was instability and constant infighting. The meetings of the District Councils were not held regularly.[3]

The control of the District Councils were often perpetuated in selected hands. Most of the Chief Executive Members and the Executive Members of the Karbi Anglong District came from only a few families related by blood.[4]

REFERENCES

1. Kumar, B.B., *Reorganization of North-East India: Facts and Documents*, pp. 20-21.
2. *Ibid.*, p. 20.
3. *Ibid.*
4. *Ibid.*

5

THE LINGUISTIC REORGANIZATION OF THE STATES

AS already discussed, the adjustment and the structural changes just after independence resulted into the formation of four categories of States in India. Merger and adjustments of the Princely States; meeting the aspirations of the Tribal people, specially on our North-Eastern Fringe, by giving some degree of local level autonomy under the provisions of the Fifth and Sixth Schedules of the Indian Constitution, etc. were the needs of the hour and the political leadership was capable enough to solve the problems. The existing arrangements, however, proved to be inadequate and fresh initiative and readjustment became necessary.

The idea of the formation of linguistic States was not new for this country. The Report of the Montagu-Chelmsford Reform favoured the formation of the linguistic States. Annie Besant, the chairperson of the Congress of Calcutta Session in 1917 opposed the idea of the formation of the linguistic States. Bal Gangadhar Tilak and Gandhiji favoured it. Gandhiji favoured the use of linguistic sensibilities of the people for mass-organization.

The All-India Congress Committee officially accepted the Principle of the 'Linguistic Reorganization of States' in its Nagpur Session in 1920. The Congress also accepted it as the basis of its own organization in 1921. The leadership of the Congress reiterated its stand in this matter before the Indian Statutory Commission of 1927 and suggested the creation of Utkal, Andhra, Sind and Karnataka on that basis.

The Nehru Committee of All-Parties Conference in 1928 forcefully supported the idea of the Reorganization of States on the Linguistic basis. The Election Manifesto of the Congress promised to create the provinces on linguistic and cultural basis during 1946.

The line of thinking of the national leaders changed just after independence in this matter. The leaders who vehemently supported the idea of the linguistic States found it difficult to sustain after independence due to the problems of real politics and administration. The Central Provinces had the Hindi and Marathi speaking people. The Bombay had Marathi, Gujarati and Kannada speakers. Similarly, the Madras had Tamil, Telugu and the Malyalam speaking people. The perceptions, interests and the emotions of the people speaking different languages differed. The leaders realised the problem. Mahatma Gandhi and Dr. B.R. Ambedkar opposed the creation of the Linguistic States at this juncture.

The Jawaharlal-Vallabhbhai Patel-Pattabhi Sitarammaiya Committee of the Indian National Congress (JVP Committee) was formed in 1948. The Committee was asked to thoroughly deliberate on the matter and to submit its findings. The Committee studied the issue and came out with its findings opposing the formation of linguistic States in India.

Another attempt was also made to solve the vexed problem. The Linguistic Provinces Commission was appointed to study the problem and to submit its findings. It was also known as Dhar Committee and was appointed by Dr. Rajendra Prasad on June 17, 1948 under the chairmanship of Justice S.N. Dhar, retired Judge of the Allahabad High Court. The other members were Dr. Pannalal (a retired ICS officer) and Jagat Narayan Lal (Member, Constituent Assembly). B.C. Banerjee (Accountant General, Bihar) was the secretary and nine Associate Members were Ramkrishna Jaju, T.A. Ramalingam, Narayan Menon, T. Subrahamanyam, K.M. Munshi, R.R. Diwakar, H.V. Pataskar, T.L. Siyode and Gopal Shrivatsa. Dhar Committee found it 'inadvisable' to reorganise the States on linguistic basis. The Constituent Assembly accepted the recommendation. Pt. Nehru opposed any move in this direction for some time. However, sentiments were highly in favour of the Linguistic States in some parts of the country and the Prime Minister had to bow down ultimately in this case.

Telugu speaking people of the then Madras Presidency wanted to have their own State just after the creation of the State of 'Bihar & Orissa' in 1912. They formed Andhra Mahasabha in 1913, just a year after the creation of Bihar & Orissa, to pursue their objective of a separate State. The dream of the Telugu speaking people to have a separate State of their own remained unfulfilled for half a century. Potti Sriramulu, veteran Congressman went on a fast unto death from October 19, 1952. He died on December 15, 1952 after 56 days of fasting. There was large-scale violence in the State and the Government of India created Andhra Pradesh on October 1, 1953. Thus Andhra Pradesh was the first State of the country created on the linguistic basis after independence.

As already stated, the British created the provinces to meet their imperial needs and to facilitate the smooth and efficient administration. This remained their sole motive in all the cases of the creation of new provinces, although Assam, Bihar, Orissa and Sindh were apparently the linguistic provinces. It is pertinent to note that the communal divide was also the aim of the British masters in their scheme of territorial reorganization. The creation of East Bengal & Assam and its annulment was not done on linguistic consideration. The East Bengal and Sind were carved out as Muslim majority States. The motive behind the creation of East Bengal and later on 'Bihar & Orissa' was to weaken the nationalist movement of Bengal.

Kannada and Malayalam speaking people got their States as a result of the recommendations of the States' Reorganization Commission. Karnataka and Kerala were formed in 1956. However, the Commission did not recommend the partition of Bombay and Punjab leading to agitations by the Marathi, Gujarati and Punjabi speaking people for their own States.

Bombay was divided in 1960 due to the prolonged agitation for the formation of Maharashtra and Gujarat. The Marathi and Gujarati speaking people got their respective States. The agitation continued for the bifurcation of the bilingual State of Punjab into Punjabi Suba and Haryana for a few more years. The Akalis agitated for the formation of Punjabi speaking Sikh majority Punjabi Suba. Saint Fateh Singh threatened self-immolation. The Parliament Committee chaired by Sardar Hukum Singh on the demand for the Punjabi Suba recommended in favour of the partition of the bilingual State into Punjabi Suba and Haryana. The two states were born in 1966. Chandigarh became a centrally administered territory. The demands for the Linguistic States almost ended. Every language listed in the eighth schedule of the constitution except Urdu and Sanskrit had atleast a State in that year.

The States' Reorganization Commission

As already stated, the demands for the creation of the Linguistic States continued after the creation of Andhra Pradesh. The Kannada speaking people were on the fore-front of such agitation. The Government ignored the demands for new States for some time. The grouping of the Indian States into groups A, B, C and D also continued for some time. However,

Prime Minister, Nehru could not ignore the demands of the people. He was a highly sensitive person and his sensitivity was responsible for the formation of States' Reorganization Commission and later on for that of the State of Nagaland.

Michael Edwardes, Nehru's political biographer, in his book on Nehru (p. 253) has mentioned about the hostile black-flag demonstration before him in Belgaum in early 1954 demanding the formation of a Kannada speaking State. The States' Reorganization Commission was announced just after that. Michael Edwardes has attributed the formation of the States' Reorganization Commission as a result of Pt. Nehru's protean political style and his abnormal sensitivity of the mood of the crowds. The same factor was, perhaps, responsible for the creation of Nagaland. It opened the flood-gate of the demands for the formation of small States in India. It is necessary to cite the episode here.

Nehru visited Kohima with Burmese Prime Minister, U. Nu in May, 1953 and the local people attempted to submit a memorandum to him during the reception meeting. Denial of which led to famous walk out from the public meeting arranged to welcome the two Prime Ministers P.D. Strecey in his *Nagaland Nightmare* (pp. 59-60) has described the incident, which I am quoting below:

> "The Nehru incident was a terrible rebuff to the Great Indian leader. From the accounts of the incident that are available, it appears that there had been some bungling over the presentation of a petition from the public to the Prime Minister. A Deputy Commissioner, apparently acting on the orders of the Chief Minister of Assam, who was present, told the deputationists that not more than three persons could submit the memorandum and that only after the public meeting. But the leaders insisted on presenting the paper in the public meeting itself, as if it was from all the people. This the authorities could not permit. In a way, they were acting correctly, as Nehru had a short time before told the Nagas that he would not hear anything more on the Naga demand for independence."
>
> "Whatever, it was, the repercussions were serious. The Prime Minister was unfortunately a little late in arriving at the meeting and the large crowd which has assembled, became restive, probably under the influence of some trouble makers. A murmuring arose to the effect that they should not wait to meet someone who had refused to receive their petition, and the assembly began to melt away. Just then the Prime Minister arrived but all the efforts of the

local officials to restrain the dispersing crowd proved in vain. They went, smacking their buttocks as a sign of rejection and Nehru with his daughter beside him watched them go. A witness who was present at the meeting records a poignant touch. Indira Gandhi agitated and speaking unwittingly into the 'live' microphone, said, in Hindi: "Father, Father, they are going away" and Nehru replied, in sombre voice, "Yes I am seeing them, I am seeing them, daughter I." It is said that Nehru was very mortified and vowed that he would never come back to Kohima. This can hardly be believed of such a magnanimous individual, but it is strange that he did not visit the Naga country from then, even upto the time of his death in May, 1964."

As stated above, the States' Reorganization Commission was set up under the chairmanship of Justice Fazl Ali in 1954 with Hriday Nath Kunjru and K.M. Pannikar as members. The formal announcement was made by Dr. Kailash Nath Katju, the then Home Minister. The Commission toured the entire length and the breadth of the country, met about 9,000 persons, considered 1,52,250 applications, memoranda, and communications and finally submitted the report after 1 year 9 months and 3 days on September 30, 1955. It had 267 printed pages.

The Commission based its recommendations on the following factors:

(a) preservation of the unity and security of the country,
(b) linguistic and cultural homogeneity,
(c) financial, economic and administrative considerations,
(d) successful implication of the five year plans.

Thus the Commission broadened the parameters for considering any unit for statehood. In spite of the factors, such as unity and integrity of the country, financial, administrative and developmental issues figuring prominently, the commission did not ignore the linguistic and cultural aspect of the reorganization. Most of the States created after reorganization, except Bombay, Punjab and Assam, were linguistically and culturally homogeneous.

The Commission suggested the creation of 16 States and 3 centrally administered territories. The Government ultimately formed 14 States (Andhra Pradesh, Assam, Bombay, Jammu & Kashmir, Kerala, Madhya Pradesh, Madras (now, Tamilnadu), Mysore (now, Karnataka), Orissa, Punjab, Rajasthan, Uttar Pradesh and West Bengal) and 6 centrally

Administered Territories (Andaman and Nicobar Islands, Delhi, Himachal Pradesh, Manipur, Tripura and Lakshadip, Minicoy & Amindivi Islands). Thus, the most cumbersome and haphazard division of the country into Part-A, Part-B, Part-C and Part-D was done away with. Rajasthan was born after the merger of Part-C States of Rajputana (erstwhile Princely States). Madhya Pradesh became the biggest State geographically by merger and permutation and combination of territories. Travancore and Cochin was a Malayalam speaking area. The Malayalam speaking areas of Madras and Mysore were added to the same giving birth to Kerala. Purulia subdivision and parts of Purnia district of Bihar went to West Bengal. Telugu and Marathi areas of Hyderabad State were merged into the States of Andhra Pradesh and Bombay respectively. Thus, reorganization was really a very fruitful and rewarding exercise. A better and cohesive picture emerged after the implementation of the recommendations of the Report of the States Reorganization Commission in 1956.

As already stated, the reorganization of States did not end after the implementation of the S.R.C. Report. Pressure mounted for the linguistic States further and the States of Maharashtra and Gujarat by the bifurcation of Bombay State and Haryana and Punjabi Suba by the bifurcation of Punjab State were born within a decade.

The situation after the implementation of the recommendations of the States' Reorganization Commission may be summed up as given below:

(i) Marathi speaking area of Madhya Pradesh and Hyderabad and Gujarati speaking Saurashtra and Kutch were added to the new and bigger Bombay State.

(ii) A new and biggest in the geographical area was the State of Madhya Pradesh consisting of the Hindi speaking areas of old Madhya Pradesh, Madhya Bharat, Vindhya Pradesh, Bhopal and certain parts of Rajasthan.

(iii) A new State of Andhra Pradesh consisting of the old territories of Andhra Pradesh and nine Telengana districts of Hyderabad was created.

(iv) A new Mysore State was created by merging the existing Group B—Mysore State, Karnataka speaking areas of Bombay and Madras, Coorg and Raichur and Beedar districts of Hyderabad.

(v) Travancore-Cochin and Malabar from Madras presidency were merged together to form the new State of Kerala.

(vi) Ajmer, PEPSU, Bilaspur and Cooch Behar were merged to the States of Rajasthan, Punjab, Himachal Pradesh and West Bengal respectively.

(vii) The State of Hyderabad, Madhya Bharat, Vindhya Pradesh, PEPSU, Saurashtra, Ajmer, Kutch, Bhopal, Bilaspur, Coorg, and Cooch Behar ceased to exist.

(viii) The categorization of Group A, B, C and D States was abolished. There was only the States and the Union Territories.

(ix) A new Union territory, called, 'the Laccadive, Minicoy & Amindivi Islands, was created. Group-C States of Manipur, Tripura, Himachal Pradesh and Delhi became Union Territories.

(x) The implementation of the S.R.C. Report generated agitation for the bifurcation of Bombay and Punjab, which resulted into the formation of Maharashtra, Gujarat, Punjab and Haryana.

6

NAGALAND AND THE SMALL STATES SYNDROME

THE formation of linguistic States did not fully settle the demands for the creation of new States. The country faced problems in the North-Eastern region due to secessionist demand in the Naga Hills district from the very beginning after independence. Initially, Nagas wanted a place in India within the State of Assam, but gradually, a section under the leadership of Phizo wanted separation from India. This development was possible due to the influence of the British administrators of the district. The moderates among the Nagas wanted to remain under India.

A considerable part of the North-Eastern region was declared backward area as per the Government of India Act, 1919. This was advised by the Montagu-Chelmsford Report of 1917. The Act of 1935 and the declaration of excluded and semi-excluded areas was the result of Simon Commission Report. The Inner Line Regulation, 1873 was an old colonial act designed to isolate the Hills and Plains of the North-East region and it had certainly the impact desired by the colonial masters.

The impact of isolationist design of the British may be seen in the absence of the freedom movement in the excluded and semi-excluded areas of the country. Needless to say that the National Movement under the leadership of Mahatma Gandhi played great role in silent emotional integration of India.

Apart from the above-mentioned attempts of isolating the hills and the plains, some British officers really aimed at the physical separation of the North-Eastern Hills of India. The efforts gained ground after the intensification of Freedom-movement under the leadership of Gandhiji. The attempt of Robert Neil Reid, the Governor of Assam to get a crown colony carved out of the hill areas, including North-East Frontier tracts, Naga Hills, Mizo Hills, Chittagong hill tracts, etc. was designed as a part of well-thought out strategy. J.H. Hutton, Deputy Commissioner of Naga Hills district, J.P. Mills, Advisor to the Governor and other subscribed to the idea of separation.

The plan of separation was again revived in 1941, when some British officials wanted to carve out North-Eastern Frontier Province comprising the hill areas of North-East India and Burma under British protection.

Andrew Clow, the Governor of Assam and Sir Reginald Coupland, a British constitutional expert favoured the formation of a Crown Colony, comprising hills of North-East India and Burma. Coupland said that 'the inhabitants of both areas are alike in race and culture, and in no sense belonged to the Indian or Burman Nation'. The takers of these ideas were many and the logic is echoed often by the protagonists of secession in North-East India.

The ill-designs and the efforts of the British officers could not bear fruits. Obviously, it was due to the fact that the British were too deeply involved in the Second World War and freedom came very soon after the War.

The historical background of our immediate colonial past played crucial role in what happened and continues to happen on our North Eastern Fringe. Unimaginative handling of the problem in Nagaland has also contributed in aggravating the problem further. The Small States Syndrome was born in India after the creation of Nagaland, the then smallest State of the Indian Union.

The insurgency in the Naga Hills district of Assam and the S.R.C. were born almost at the same time. The autonomy movement was born slightly earlier. The autonomy movement in Naga Hills resulted ultimately into the formation of Nagaland State which opened the flood-gate of demands for the formation of States of any size and population, overlooking the factors of economic viability. The following points are worth noting in this connection:

(i) Nagaland was the first State of the Union, which was not formed on linguistic lines. The factors considered to be essential for the formation of a State by the S.R.C. were also ignored.

(ii) The Indian leaders and the S.R.C. believed in bigger States, Nagaland was the first State with comparatively very small population and size.

(iii) It made the experiment on district level autonomy under the provisions of the Sixth Schedule of the Constitution practically ineffective.

(iv) Insurgency and underground movement preceded the formation of the State. The matter was highly propagated that the statehood was granted due to the fear of gun. The wrong signal that the violence pays had many takers. Mizos followed the example and Mizo Hills district ultimately became Mizoram State. Ghisingh threatened and he continues to threaten even after getting autonomy for Darjeeling Hills.

(v) It was the first State created on ethnic lines and disturbed the age old ethnic harmony of the region. Assam which was one of the most peaceful parts of the country became the most disturbed one and continues to be so even today. Ethnicity was linked for the first time with the political loaf and the takers were numerous.

(vi) The criteria of economic viability was ignored. The running of the State became affair of power without responsibility, the loaf without labour, as the State was to run mainly on the grants received from the Consolidated Fund of India.

The nation ceased to question the criteria of State formation. Public became confused. The process was intensified by the journalists, politicians and the career elites. The process of the bulkanization of Assam which started after the formation of Nagaland continues.

The formation of small States did not follow uniform pattern. The trends and the pattern, the methods employed for achieving statehood, etc. differed considerably. The same may be categorised as given below:

(i) The underground movements and the violence preceded the formation of the States of Nagaland and Mizoram.

(ii) Meghalaya achieved statehood through non-violent peaceful means. The experiments of the autonomy within the State of Assam failed. The United Khasi and Jaintia Hills district and the Garo Hills district of Assam formed the State of Meghalaya.

(iii) The erstwhile Princely States of Manipur and Tripura became full-fledged States of the Union, as the area, population and the economic viability ceased to be the valid criteria for the statehood.

(iv) Arunachal Pradesh followed the course of gradual and smooth evolution. It has big geographical area and small population.

(v) Sikkim became a State after its merger into Indian Union.

(vi) The people of Goa wanted to merge their State into Maharashtra and voted a pro-merger party, Maharashtrawadi Gomantaka Dal, to power. The Government of India ignored the wishes of the people. 'Goa, Daman and Diu' remained a centrally administered territory for considerable period. Finally Goa became a full-fledged State of the Indian Union. 'Daman & Diu' was made the Union Territory.

A very brief sketch of the history of the formation of the North-Eastern States is given below:

The Naga hills District Tribal Council was formed in 1945 to work for the rehabilitation and reconstruction of the war devastated areas of Naga Hills. The initiative for the same was taken by C.R. Pawsey, the then Deputy Commissioner of the district. The Council soon converted itself into a political platform of the Nagas, named Naga National Council. The Council submitted a Memorandum drafted on June 19, 1945 to His Majesty's Government. The relevant portion of the same is quoted below:

> "The Naga National Council stands for the solidarity of the Naga tribes including those of the unadministered areas."
> "The Council strongly protests against the grouping of Assam with Bengal."
> "The Naga Hills should be constitutionally included in an autonomous Assam in a free India with local autonomy and duly safeguarded for the interests of the Nagas."

The Sixth Schedule of the Constitution of India provided local autonomy to the Nagas under autonomous Assam in free India. However, the Sixth Schedule was never given a trial in the Naga Hills district as Naga National Council became the platform of the extremist Nagas under the chairmanship of A.Z. Phizo just before the independence.

The Naga National Council (NNC) demanded self-determination of the Nagas. They based their argument on the following points:

(i) Ethnic distinctiveness,
(ii) Distinct social life, way of living, laws and customs, etc.
(iii) Different religion—Animism and Christianity.

The Nagas National Council signed a nine-point agreement with Hydari, the Government of Assam, when the latter visited Kohima on

June 26, 1947. The agreement proved to be a still-born baby. The NNC started civil disobedience in early 1950s. The Phizo was very much inspired by the creation of Pakistan. If India could be divided to form a Muslim State, then why not for a Christian State? The very platform which wanted status of a district for the Naga area, voiced the demand for self-determination as soon as it became known that the division of the country was inevitable and Pakistan was going to be a reality. The tenacities of Zinnah and Phizo are comparable.

The following happenings of the early 1952, boosted the morale and image of the secessionists. At the same time, it demoralised the administration:

(i) Non-participation of the Nagas in the District Council formation.
(ii) Boycott of 1952 election by the Nagas.
(iii) Successful plebiscite in favour of Naga independence. It was conducted by Phizo from May to August, 1952. One interesting feature of the plebiscite was that the boxes for 'Yes' and 'No' votes were kept in different rooms, exposing the identity of 'No' voters to the imminent danger. Thus, it was natural that most of the Nagas voted in favour of the Naga independence.

Some of the activities of the hard-liners devised as a part of their civil-disobedience movement are given below:

(i) Non-payment of the house-tax,
(ii) Boycotting national and official celebrations,
(iii) Non-co-operation with the Government in its development schemes,
(iv) Refusal to supply food-items and labour to the touring officers,
(v) Return of red blankets—the badges of authority by the Gaon-Buras to the Deputy Commissioner.
(vi) Forced resignations of the school teachers and forced withdrawal of the students from the schools. It may be pointed out that the seniormost National Council leaders arranged for the best education of their children and wanted other to do otherwise.

Naga National Council (NNC) took full advantage of the communication gap between the Nagas and other countrymen and of their ignorance about each other. The Nagas easily believed that the Indians may rob them of their land and resources, make them slaves and convert them to Hinduism.

Very soon non-violence gave way to violent agitation. Army and the police retaliated, the people suffered. Most important colleagues of Phizo, such as, Sakhrie and Jasokie (both from his village, Khonoma) deserted him. Sakhrie was cruelly murdered. There was strong public resentment.

The underground Nagas formed the Federal Government of Nagaland in March 1956. They framed their Constitution. Some articles of their Constitution are given below:

> "Nagaland is a people's sovereign republic. This have been so from the time immemorial. There will be a parliament with 100 Tatars (M.Ps.), the President will be elected by the people and his cabinet will consist of 15 Kilonsers (ministers)."
>
> "Nagaland will maintain permanent military neutrality. There will be no army for the maintenance of law and order. There will be a department of Home-guards headed by a Chief to function in a dual capacity of police and patriotic soldiers."
>
> "Land belongs to the people and it will remain so. There will be no land-tax, and other forms of taxation will be formulated by different administrative units."
>
> "All forms of trade, business, industry, transport and other public utility will be free and will be in the hands of the people."
>
> "Religion will be free."
>
> "Each Naga village is a republic in its own right. Each Naga family or tribe occupies its own distinct region, and shall continue as before to exercise full authority over its own affairs, including land, community, organization, social and religious practices and customs."
>
> "Men and women above 22 years of age, will have equal right of voting." "There will be equal wages for equal work irrespective of sex."

Provisions were made for the appointment on various posts, such as the Angs (Governors), Judges, Ambassadors, etc. Their Constitution provided for a Federal Court also. Commander-in-Chief of the military organization of home-guards was appointed. Arms and ammunitions left over by the army during the Second World War were collected by the insurgents. Some arms and ammunitions were ceased from the individuals or captured in the raids.

The sober Naga voices started being heard very soon. Three Naga People's Conventions were organized one after another. These conventions were attended by large number of Nagas from every tribe. The conventionists wanted autonomy under the frame-work of the Constitution of India. In the meantime, three Nagas were elected unopposed to the Assam Assembly in 1957 general elections and one of them was made a Deputy Minister. However, they resigned when the Prime Minister Nehru accepted the demand of the first Naga People's Convention and an Union Territory, named, Naga Hills Tuensang Area (NHTA) was formed on August 1, 1957 by merging Naga Hills district of Assam and Tuensang division of North East Frontier Agency (NEFA).

The second and the third Naga People's conventions were held in May, 1958 and October, 1959 respectively. They formulated certain demands. Pt. Nehru was sympathetic. He accepted most of their demands, which included the formation of Nagaland State. Nehru conceded their demand. A bill was passed under the provision of Article 3 of the Constitution. Nagaland became the sixteenth State of the Union on December 1, 1963. Special provisions were made under Article 371A for the protection of the land and natural resources and the customary laws and usages of the Nagas.

7

THE EXPERIMENTS OF A STATE WITHIN A STATE: THE CASE OF MEGHALAYA

A series of experiments were made before finally Meghalaya became a full-fledged State of the Indian Union. The area enjoyed internal autonomy under the provisions of the Sixth Schedule. It had District Councils in the Garo Hills and the United Khasi and Jaintiya Hills Districts.

The Hill State Demand

A conference of the people of the autonomous hill districts of Assam was called by Williamson Sangma on October 6, 1954 at Tura to consider the demand of a hill State. It was decided to submit a memorandum to the States' Reorganisation Commission for the formation of a separate 'Eastern Hill State'. Accordingly, the memorandum was submitted to the SRC for the creation of the new State. The memorandum mainly emphasised the following points.[1]

(i) The people of the hills and the plains differed from each other.
(ii) The attempt of the Assamese people to impose their language and culture on the hill tribes,
(iii) The Assamese dominance in the legislature and the services, and
(iv) The autonomy granted under the Sixth Schedule was not adequate.

The formation of the Eastern Hill State formed the agenda of another conference also. The conference which was convened by B.M. Roy, the Chief Executive member of the Khasi & Jaintiya Hills District

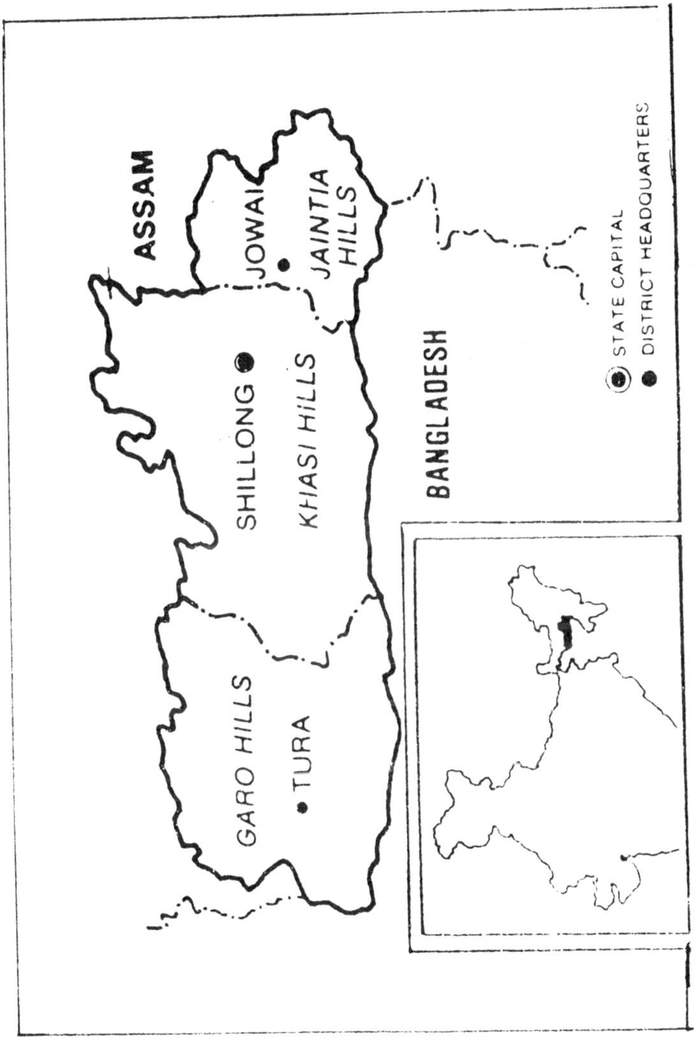

A Sketch Map MAP 7.1 : Meghalaya

Council and attended by the executive members of all the District Councils except that of the Mikir Hills District Council, discussed the following:[2]

(i) Formation of the Eastern Hill State,
(ii) More autonomy to the District Councils by amending the Sixth Schedule,
(iii) English as the State language to be replaced by Hindi in due course.

The members of the North Cachar Hills and Lushai Hills wanted greater autonomy for the districts rather than for the new State.

The issue of separate State was made the election issue in 1957. The Tribal Union, U.M.F.O. and the Garo National Union captured ten seats and the Congress only one seat in the Assam Legislative Assembly from the Hill Districts. The reconciliation move resulted into Eastern India Tribal Union joining the Chaliha Ministry. The demand for separate State was almost given up. The Tribal Affairs Advisory Committee advised the amendment of the Sixth Schedule to give more powers to the District Councils.

The Birth of All-Party Hill Leaders Conference

The Official Languages Bill was introduced in the Assam Assembly on October 18, 1960. The hill leaders of all the districts except that of the Mikir Hills and the North Cachar Hills districts, opposed the introduction of the bill vehemently. They formed All-Party Hill Leaders Conference on November 2, 1960 and decided to fight for the hill State by peaceful and constitutional methods. The new party demanded the creation of a 'North East Frontier State' consisting of the tribal areas of Assam, Manipur and Tripura . They demanded the following for the new State:

(i) A separate Governor,
(ii) A Council of Ministers,
(iii) 60-member unicameral Assembly,
(iv) Three Rajya Sabha members,
(v) One Lok Sabha member from each district and two from NEFA,
(vi) Separate High Court,
(vii) A separate University,
(viii) A Public Service Commission,

(ix) Retention and strengthening of the District and Regional Councils, and
(x) English as the State language.

The APHLC delegation met Pt. Nehru. He assured them of the continuance of English in the secretariat, use of medium of instruction of their choice, maximum internal autonomy, sufficient budget for development and their representation in the National Development Council meetings. He was against the smaller States due to their economic non-viability. The Home Minister also raised certain issues such as the geographical non-contiguity of the districts and the complementary nature of the economy of the hills and the plains. The Prime Minister put forwarded the Scottish Plan for them.

The Scottish Plan

The Scottish Plan was envisaged to provide more autonomy to the Hill Districts of Assam under the frame-work of the State The main features of the said plan were the following:

(i) Regional Committees consisting of all the MLAs from the Hill districts with certain powers.
(ii) Statutory State Council for looking after planning and development funds.
(iii) The Committee of MLAs from hills under the Cabinet Minister in-charge of the Hill Affairs to scrutinize the applicability and extension of legislations to the hill areas.
(iv) A cabinet Minister and one or more Deputy Ministers from among the MLAs from the hills to be the in-charge of subjects concerning the hill area.
(v) Separate budget for the hill area.
(vi) More powers to the District Councils.
(vii) The Governor's verdict to be final in case of the disagreement between the Assam Assembly and the Regional Committee.
(viii) The appointment of the Commission of Enquiry.

The Scottish Plan was not accepted by the tribals. It did not tackle the language problem. The proposed Statutory State Council was just like the earlier Advisory Council, which did not satisfy them. There was enough scope for conflict and friction due to non-separation of administration.

The APHLC fought 1962 Assembly election on Scottish Plan issue and won most of the seats. APHLC asked its MLAs to resign when new State was not formed after the elections, but many MLAs defied party directive and did not resign. It lost 1963 by-election. Gradually, the party shrunk only to two districts of Assam, namely, the United Khasi and Jaintiya Hills and the Garo Hills districts. The Prime Minister offered a new plan of autonomy for them under the Nehru Plan.

The Nehru Plan

Many provisions of the Nehru Plan were same as we find in the Scottish Plan. Some important provisions of the same are given below:

- (i) Amendment of the Sixth Schedule to give more powers to the District and the Regional Councils.
- (ii) A Regional Council for all the hill districts; the law affecting hill areas to be referred to the Council for approval.
- (iii) Each hill district to have one MP (Lok Sabha) and one MLA for every 40,000 population.
- (iv) A Cabinet Minister in-charge of the hill area, a Minister of State and one or two Deputy Ministers.
- (v) Control of Hill Ministry over education, agriculture, horticulture, forests, health and the administration of justice.
- (vi) Separate wing of secretariat for hill affairs.
- (vii) The Hill Minister shall (a) have control over making of plans; (b) have access to Planning Commission; (c) Control expenditure on the subjects under him; (d) be responsible for the preparation of budget with the help of a Financial Advisor; (e) central grants given under Article 275 and revenue collected in the hills; (f) regulate appointments, postings, and transfers under his charge; and (g) determine the official language.
- (viii) Continuance of constitutional provisions safeguarding the interests of the hill people;
- (ix) Provision for separate university.
- (x) Measures to be taken to quicken development.
- (xi) Appointment of a Commission to work out details of hill people accept the plan.

The Nehru Plan provided for the infringement of the rights of the Assam Legislature and the Chief Minister. The Cabinet birth for the hill people was too less. The plains people could have practically no say in the affairs of the hills, whereas the hill MLAs had every say in the affairs of the plains as the MLAs of the Assam Legislature. The Plan was accepted by the tribal people after such bickerings and the Pataskar Commission was appointed to work out the details.

Pataskar Commission

The Pataskar Commission did not recommend for a separate wing of the secretariat; did not recommend full authority in the matters of planning, budgeting and control of expenditure in the hands of the hill people. It recommended the strengthening of the District Councils. Thus the recommendations fell far short of the Nehru Plan. The recommendations were rejected by the tribal leaders and accepted by the Assam Government. The Pataskar Commission failed to bring results. Further attempts were made to solve the vexed problem one after another after the failure of this attempt.

The Nanda Committee Recommendations and the Sub-state

A Cabinet Committee was formed under the chairmanship of Gulzari Lal Nanda, the then Union Home Minister to work out the solution. The Nanda Committee recommended the formation of Meghalaya Sub-state with separate legislature and separate Council of Ministers under Assam. The Plan was rejected by the hill leaders.

Federal Plan

It was the brain-child of Vishnu Sahay, the Governor. The plan suggested the formation of Federated States of Assam including Hill States, Manipur, Tripura and if possible, NEFA. Equal status for all the federating units was envisaged. Equal status for the hills and plains was suggested for the first time under this plan. The plan did not evoke positive response.

Mehta Plan

This plan suggested maximum district level autonomy. The Mikir Hills and North Cachar Hills District Councils welcomed the plan. The APHLC rejected it. The Party threatened to direct action on December

20, 1967. The threat was repeated. The Government of India announced the plan of reorganization.

The important points of the plan of reorganization is given below:

1. The autonomous State of Meghalaya shall consist of the Garo Hills and the United Khasi & Jaintiya Hills districts of Assam. The North Cachar and the Mikir Hills were free to join the Hill State if 2/3 members of their District Councils vote for the same.
2. The Hill State was to have a legislative assembly and council of ministers.
3. It would have power to levy and collect taxes on minerals, passengers, goods, land revenue, excise duty, agricultural income tax and entertainment tax.
4. Fifty-nine subjects of the State list was to be transferred to hill State and remaining seven including State highways, major irrigational and flood control projects, etc., Hydro-electric projects and navigation to Assam. Some concurrent list subjects, such as, the conservation of forests, agricultural schemes of common benefit, acquisition and requisition of property were also given to the Hill State.
5. The executive power and the subjects assigned to the hill State shall be co-extensive.
6. The bills passed by the legislature would need the Governor's assent.
7. There would be a joint cadre of All-India Services. Police and Public order list would remain with Assam to enable the State to maintain unified administration.
8. The hill State would continue to have representation in the Assam Legislative Assembly and Cabinet. The Assembly and the Standing Committees of the same shall have its jurisdiction over subjects of common interest in the plains.
9. There shall be common High Court, Public Service Commission and the Electricity Board for Assam and the Hill State.
10. The District Councils would be given more powers.
11. The Shillong would continue to be the capital of both the States.
12. The Autonomous State would continue to be the part of Assam.

The Assam Government did not accept the plan on the plea that it would endanger unity, integrity and security of the country. The APHLC accepted the plan on January 28, 1969.

The autonomous State of Meghalaya was formed after the Constitution (Twenty-second Amendment) Act, 1969 received the assent of the President on September 25, 1969. A new article (Article 244A) was inserted in the constitution as per Article 2 of the Act. Article 275 of the Constitution was amended, which empowered the new State to use the grants-in-aid received from the Consolidated Fund of India. Article 371B was inserted in the Constitution of India as a new Article.

The Mikir Hills and the North Cachar Hills did not join the autonomous State. The Mizos did not remain the part of APHLC from an early date. Thus, only United Khasi & Jaintiya Hills and the Garo Hills remained with the new Autonomous State of Meghalaya. The Autonomous State of Meghalaya was inaugurated on April 2, 1970.

The experiment proved to be futile. The Meghalaya became full-fledged State within two years along with Manipur and Tripura after the North-Eastern Area (Reorganization) Act, 1971 was passed by the Parliament and received the assent of the President.

REFERENCES

1. Kumar, B.B. *Re-organization of North-East India: Fact and Documents*; p. 37.
2. *Ibid.*

8

EMERGENCE OF OTHER SMALL STATES IN INDIA

THE 'Big State' norm was broken after the creation of the State of Nagaland with small size and population. The economic viability was not questioned after that and many States emerging after that State were smaller in area as well as population. Most of the small States except Goa were economically non-viable and needed heavy doses of funds from the Consolidated Fund of India for their Plan as well as Non-plan expenses.

Most of the small States emerged in North-East India after its reorganization. Manipur and Tripura were the Princely States during the pre-independence period. Mizoram was a district of Assam, called the Lushai Hills. Garo Hills and the United Khasi & Jaintia Hills emerged as Meghalaya.

Only two small States, located in other parts of the country were Sikkim and Goa. Both the States were merged in India and attained statehood in due course of time.

The pattern and the trends of the formation of small States in India differed considerably. We may discuss the same in the succeeding paragraphs of this chapter.

The Mizos followed the Nagas in many respects in their autonomy demands. A section of them also claimed secession under the leadership of Lal Denga. They, like the Nagas, followed the path of insurgency, though insurgency in their area was started very late.

The armed rebellion was started in Mizo Hills district of Assam on February 28,1966. It, however, lasted only for a very brief period. The Government of India resorted to the application of the Assam Disturbed Areas Act, 1955 and the Armed Forces (Assam and Manipur) Special Power Act, 1958. The army started operation immediately to flush out the rebels. The hard-core underground retired to the deep forests. The

Army also worked out Operation Security by regrouping of the villages. The aim of the regrouping of the villages was:

(i) to facilitate effective military operation against the rebels,
(ii) to segregate the rebels from the masses.
(iii) to provide protection to the villagers,
(iv) to provide social service to the community.
(v) to facilitate economic development, and
(vi) to provide communication facilities.

The regrouping of villages helped the villagers, no doubt, but, not without suffering to them. It helped the Army in segregating the rebels from the masses and in effective combing operation.

The Mizos accepted the constitutional provisions of the Sixth Schedule and had their District Councils. They always voted for the Mizo Union party which was against the secession of the Mizo Hills from India. Mizo National Front under the leadership of Lal Denga openly preached secession, but was defeated in the District Council elections and general elections. The avoidable neglect by the Assam Government and the petty politics of the Assam Congress leaders was responsible for the people's anger and alienation, and their sympathy for the Mizo National Front (MNF). Whenever the bamboo flowers in Mizoram, the rat population multiplies, resulting into famine. Mizos call it 'Mautam Tampui (mau = bamboo, tampui = havoc of famine). There was one such famine in 1959, Government of Assam was forewarned, but lax relief operation resulted into death and sufferings. The people were angry with the Assam Government.

The Mizo National Famine Front was formed in 1959. Lal Denga was the Secretary. Relief work popularised by Lal Denga. Abolition of chieftainship, misuse of the compensation money and their pauperization made them a disgruntled lot. The discharged men of second battalion of the Assam regiment were not rehabilitated and joined the armed wing of the rebels. Unemployed youth also became their active sympathisers. Proper economic planning lacked in the district and the people became the prey to MNF propaganda.

Lack of fore-sight and dynamism, and vacillation on the part of the then Chief Minister of Assam aggravated the problem. The MNF was preaching secession; preparing for armed revolt, and yet continued to talk about non-violence and deceive him. Mizo Union leaders and the District Council maintained good relation with the Congress. However, they joined All-Party Hill Leaders Conference and demanded a Hill State and later on a State for the Mizos, after they differed from the Assam leaders on the issue of making Assamese the State language of the State. The Chief Minister helped MNF to weaken the Mizo Union. The country and the State of Assam paid the price for his short-sighted action.

It has already been mentioned that Mizo National Famine Front was opened in 1959. It was converted into Mizo National Front, a political party, on October 22, 1961. It preached secession without fear of action from the Government. MNF submitted a memorandum to the Prime Minister on October 30,1965. It said:

> "Mizos from time immemorial lived in complete independence without foreign interference, Chiefs of the different clans ruled over separate hills and valleys with supreme authority and their administration was very much like that of Greek city states of the past . . . they are a distinct nation, created and moulded and nurtured by God and Nature. The Mizos had never been under Indian Government. . . ."
>
> "solely (due) to their political immaturity, ignorance and lack of consciousness of their fate, the representatives of the Mizo Union choose integration with free India."
>
> "During fifteen years of contact and association with India, the Mizo people had not been able to feel at home with Indians, or in India, nor have they been able to feel that their joys and sorrows have really ever been shared by India. They do not feel, therefore, Indians. Being created a separate nation, they cannot go against the nature to cross barriers of nationality. They refused to occupy a place within India as they consider it to be unworthy of their national dignity and harmful to the interests of their posterity."
>
> "The only aspiration and the cry is the creation of Mizoram, a free and sovereign State to Govern itself to work out her own destiny and to formulate her own foreign policy."
>
> "Though Mizos are head-hunters and belong to a martial race, they will adopt non-violent methods if independence is not granted."

It is very clear from the latter developments that they talked about non-violence only to deceive the Government.

The MNF came out with a Declaration of Independence after their capture of Aizawl. It sounded somewhat like the 'Declaration of American War of Independence'. It reads:

"In the course of history, it becomes invariably necessary for mankind to assume their social, economic and political status to which the law of Nature's God entitle them. We hold this truth to be self-evident that all men are created equal and that they are endowed with inalienable fundamental human rights and dignity of human persons and to secure these rights, governments are instituted among men deriving their just powers from the consent of the governed and whenever any form of government becomes destructive of them, it is the right of the people to alter, change, modify and abolish it and institute a new government laying its foundation on such forms as to them shall seem most likely to effect their rights and dignity. The Mizos created and moulded into a nation and nurtured as such by Nature's God, have been intolerably dominated by the people of India in contravention to the laws of nature."

The Mizo underground rebels declared the formation of Mizoram Sawrkar (Government), their National Judiciary, National Army, etc.

The role model of Laldenga and the MNF was Phizo and the NNC. They received inspiration from them and were encouraged by the formation of Nagaland. Other factors accelerated their move.

Low-key insurgency continued even after crushing the rebellion. The long international border was a favourable factor for the underground Mizos. Pakistan was always helping them. It was a very low intensity proxy war for them. However, government intensified that developmental efforts. The desirability of awarding Union Territory status was felt. Mizoram was made Union Territory on January 21, 1972, as per the provision of the North-Eastern Areas (Reorganization) Act, 1971. It got its own Legislative Assembly and the Councils of Ministers.

Initiatives were taken by the Mizoram U.T. Ministry's to bring MNF to conference table. An accord was signed between the Union Home Secretary and the MNF chief, Laldenga on July 1, 1976. The accord could not be implemented, MNF resumed hostility against the security forces, civil officials and non-Mizos Laldenga was arrested and the MNF and its allied organisations were banned.

Fresh efforts by Mizoram Pradesh Congress Committee(I) failed due to the demand of 'Greater Mizoram' and Jammu & Kashmir type safeguards by Laldenga.

Lalthanhawla became the Chief Minister of the Congress Ministry in Mizoram in 1984. He resumed the peace efforts. MNF also wanted peace, Laldenga was called back from London. A Memorandum of settlement was signed between R.D. Pradhan, Union Home Secretary; Laldenga, MNF chief; and Lalkhama, Chief Secretary, Government of Mizoram. The MNF deleted the clause of 'Independence and secession from India' and other objectionable clauses and disbanded the MNA (Underground Mizo Army). The MNF and MNA cadres surrendered with arms and ammunition. Steps were taken to rehabilitate the surrendered persons.

The Government of India took steps to confer statehood on Mizoram. It became a State after the State of Mizoram Act, 1986 and the Constitution (53rd Amendment) Act were passed by the Parliament.

Mizoram followed the pattern of Nagaland in its journey to the statehood. Other States of North-Eastern region followed independent patterns.

Manipur and Tripura were princely States before independence. They became Part-C States on January 22, 1950, as per the provision of Part-C State Act, 1950. The States' Reorganization Commission recommended their merger with Assam, but the Government of India did not implement the recommendation of the SRC in this case and allowed their separate identities. The formation of Nagaland with lesser population and comparable geographical area ensured their separate identities in future also. They were given their 30 membered Territorial Councils in 1956 as per Territorial Council Act, 1956. Both the states became Union Territories in 1963 as per the provisions of Union Territories Act, 1963.

The statehood was conferred on the two States in January, 1972 as per North-Eastern (Reorganization) Act, 1971.

Arunachal Pradesh became a distinct administrative unit in 1874 as per regulation 3 of 1873. Government of India (Excluded and Partially excluded Areas) Order, 1936 provided for the administration of the area, which was vested in the Governor of Assam. Its name was changed from North East Frontier Tract to North East Frontier Agency (NEFA) by the North-East Frontier Areas (Administration) Regulation, 1954. The area became widely known after the Chinese Aggression in 1962.

Democratic institutions were introduced in the State on the recommendation of the Erring Committee Report. The North East Frontier Agency Panchayat Raj Regulation, 1967 passed as per the recommendation of the Erring Committee Report provided for the three-tier system of local self-Government starting from village through block to district level. There was provision for the establishment of the Village Council, Anchal Samiti and the Zilla Parishad.

Representatives from the Zilla Parishads formed the Agency Council comprising of 20 members—4 each from the five districts.

The Agency achieved Union Territory status in January, 1972 after the North-Eastern Areas (Reorganization) Act, 1971 was passed by the Parliament.

The people of Arunachal Pradesh also wanted to have their State after the grant of statehood to Mizoram. The Government of India conceded very promptly. The Arunachal Pradesh Bill, 1986 and the Constitution (Fifty-fifth Amendment) Bill, were introduced in the Lok Sabha in December, 1986 and passed. Rajiv Gandhi inaugurated Arunachal Pradesh as the 24th State of the Indian Union in 1987. The evolution of Arunachal Pradesh as a State of the Union was a very smooth affair indeed.[1]

The creation of Meghalaya was a most drawn out affair with a lot of experimentation. It involved the experiment of having a State within a State. On the whole, it was a non-violent and fully constitutional struggle. Meghalaya was carved out of Assam. We have discussed about the same in the previous chapter. Meghalaya, which became a State through peaceful and non-violent means without shedding blood was inaugurated on April 2, 1970.[2]

Sikkim is the smallest State of the Union, both in terms of size and population. The Indo-Sikkim Treaty, 1950 affirmed India's authority over Sikkim.[3] It may be pointed out that Sikkim remained a member of the Chamber of Princes and therefore under the British Paramountcy during the pre-independence period. The State merged with the Indian Union in 1975 and became its 22nd State.[4]

REFERENCES

1. Kumar, B.B., *Re-organization of North-East India: Facts and Documents*, pp. 46-56.
2. *Ibid.*, p. 45.
3. Singh, K. S., *People of India, Sikkim*, p. 2.
4. *Ibid.*, p. 3.

OPENING THE NEW CHAPTER

9

THE STATEHOOD FOR UTTARAKHAND

THE speculation about the future of eight hill districts of Uttar Pradesh ended after the Prime Minister's announcement from the ramparts of Red Fort on August15, 1996, of the Centre's decision to carve out the separate State of Uttarakhand. The demand for the separate State of Uttarakhand is an old one. However, it did not have the strong popular support due to the following reasons:

(i) The State of Uttar Pradesh has six regions and therefore, there is no hegemony of any particular region.
(ii) The Uttarakhand region gave three most powerful Chief Ministers—Sarvashri G.B. Pant, H.N. Bahuguna and N.D. Tiwari to the State. Therefore, the allegation to keep the region backward cannot be labelled against the politicians of other regions.
(iii) The appeal of the colonial theory of 'core-fringe conflict' has no appeal in the region due to strong national feeling.
(iv) The region has witnessed healthy movements, like Chipko Movement, movement against prohibition, etc. with due impact on the positivist thinking of the people. Deliberate distancing of communities for forced ethnic identity formation, as we witness in North-East, is not possible in Uttarakhand.
(v) The powerful leaders from Uttarakhand, such as, G.B. Pant opposed the division of Uttar Pradesh.

The States' Reorganization Commission did not recommend the formation of the State of Uttarakhand.

The Uttarakhand consists of the districts of Nainital, Almora, Pithoragarh and Chamoli of the Kumaon division and Dehradun, Pauri, Uttarkashi and Tehri districts of Garhwal division. Total area of the region is 51,082 sq. kms. and total population according to 1991 census

A Sketch Map

MAP 9.1 : Uttarakhand Region, U.P.

is 58,74,353. The districts are among the most undeveloped districts of Uttar Pradesh and among the 72 most backward districts of the country.

Uttarakhand Kranti Dal

A regional party, named, Uttarakhand Kranti Dal (UKD) raised the demand for separate Uttarakhand State in the Assembly elections of Uttar Pradesh in 1977. The Party aimed at liberating illegally occupied central Terai land from outsiders; ouster of outsiders from the fruit belt and imposition of land ceiling laws to prevent the big farmers from exploiting the people. The UKD won the Almora seat in 1980 U.P. Assembly election. It was never a political force of great reckoning in the Northern Uttar Pradesh hills.

The Present Phase of the Agitation

The announcement of the 27 per cent job reservation by Mulayam Singh Government for OBC did not evoke much resentment in the hills of Uttar Pradesh. However, the reservation in educational institutions evoked anger and resentment leading to Uttarakhand Movement. The anti-reservation movement was started on August 2, 1994 with a fast unto death by seven leaders of the UKD in Pauri district. The violence broke out and spread from Pauri to Kumaon and then to the Nainital foothills, when police applied force to end the fast. The OBC constitute only two to five per cent population of the U.P. hills. The SC and ST constitute 20 per cent of the population. Thus the total population of the SC, ST and OBC does not exceed 25 per cent in that area, whereas the total reserved seats for them in the educational institutions was 50 per cent. There was a clause that in the event of the reserved seats not being filled, a waiting period of 20 days was to be allowed to enable the candidates from the plains to avail the benefit of admission against the vacant posts. Thus there was fear of heavy influx of the students from the plains to the educational institutions of the hills. The people feared that they would find it difficult to get the educational facilities for their children in that case. The nature of economy—lack of industry, scant agricultural and tourist facilities—increased the fear of the people about their future.

The agitation and public resentment gradually took momentum and the movement for separate State was started in Uttarakhand. The situation changed drastically and there was hardening of attitude after October 2, 1994 Muzaffarnagar incident in which the Uttarakhand rallyists going to Delhi for demanding the State were stopped and brutally assaulted by the police; many persons were killed and the women raped. The CBI later on confirmed it. It is an irony that Mulayam Singh Government got the statehood resolution passed in the U.P. Legislative Assembly for the Uttarakhand after the incident. It was the second resolution passed by the U.P. Legislature for the purpose. The first one was done during the previous regime.

BJP and the Socialist Party favoured the statehood. The Congress (I) neither opposed nor favoured it. The Congress (I) initially wanted to sell the idea of the Autonomous Council. However, there was no taker of the same. Later on Congress (I) favoured Union Territory status.

It is pertinent to note that the movement for Statehood slowed down after some time due to the U.P. Governor Motilal Vora's announcement that the State Government would open the 27 per cent quota reserved for 'Other Backward Castes (OBCs), in Uttarakhand to all the non-Scheduled Castes and non-Scheduled Tribes residents. The Scheduled Castes and Scheduled Tribes have already their reserved quotas there. The Governor justified his action on the basis of a series of court judgements including May 31, 1995 ruling of the Allahabad High Court.[1] The Allahabad High Court stayed the ruling on reservation for Uttarakhand. As a result, the agitation petered out. Finally, the court ruled that the entire region could be declared "socially, economically and educationally backward." This gave fresh impetus to the movement.[2] After acceptance of the court's ruling by the State Government, which says that a region's backwardness will entitle its residents for the OBC quota, U.P. becomes the first State in the country to use the socio-economic rather than the caste criteria to determine categories eligible for reservation.[3] Other backward regions of the country may also claim the benefit of this criteria in future.

As stated above, there was a proposal to set up a Special Development Authority for Uttarakhand, which would be essentially a 'Hill Development Council' on the pattern of Darjeeling Gorkha Hill Development Council.[4] There was further development in this matter and the proposal to award Union Territory status to the region was considered as a further step.

The draft proposal of the Union Territory outlined a three-tier system with Lt. Governor in Council, a 14-member Advisory Council and a 42-member representative institution. The features of the Darjeeling Gorkha Hill Council and that of the former Union Territory of Goa and Delhi (National Capital Region) were taken and adjusted to give a new frame.[5] There are wide differences on the issue of the selection of the capital of the region between the Garhwal and Kumaon divisions. The Uttarakhand leaders sorted out the problem by selecting a place called 'Gairsain' on the borders of Garhwal and Kumaon to be the capital of the new political unit. They named it Chandra Nagar in memory of the independence struggle hero Chandra Singh Garhwali, who was a *Havildar* in the British Army and had refused to fire on unarmed people demanding India's independence.[6]

The announcement of the Centre's decision to form Uttarakhand has put an end to the speculation about the future set-up in U.P. hills. However, it did not evoke the expected enthusiasm. The suspicion in public mind was so much that slogans like "*Pahle rajya, phir chunav*" appeared overnight on the walls of the U.P. hills without erasing the previous slogan "*Rajya nahin, chunav nahin.*"[7] One reason of the apprehension and mistrust of the people about the sincerity of the Prime Minister was the timing of the announcement, which was done just before the elections.

The sudden announcement of the statehood has raised certain questions. One question is, why Uttarakhand only when violent agitations are going on for statehood in other parts of the country also? The U.P. election was at hand. The importance of 19 Assembly seats from Uttarakhand in U.P. legislature weighed heavily in poll arithmetics of the Prime Minister. The U.P. elections were fast turning into a prestige issue and the Prime Minister "with one brilliant stroke" dashed the political ambition of his rivals.[8] Ofcourse, the election results have amply shown that he miserably failed in his attempt. The thought prevailing at the particular time was, ". . . similar demands for Jharkhand, Bodoland and others can wait for the time being. It is U.P. that is going to the polls. . . ."[9]

Other important questions may also be asked at this juncture. How was it possible for the Prime Minister of a minority Government to take such a vital decision without consulting other political parties and the Parliament? Why the questions related to economic viability and other parameters were not discussed before the announcement? The answers of these questions are not difficult to find.

K.M. Pannikkar was one of the members of the States' Reorganization Commission. He gave a dissenting note in the SRC report and strongly pleaded for the formation of Agra State by the bifurcation of Uttar Pradesh for improving the administrative efficiency of the State. He supported his contention by giving a lot of facts and figures. He pleaded for the inclusion of Agra, Rohilkhand, Jhansi and Meerut divisions minus the districts of Dehradun and Pilibhit in the proposed Agra State. Even Pannikkar did not propose the formation of Uttarakhand. Pannikkar was snubbed for his suggestion. Both Pt. Jawaharlal Nehru and Govind Ballabh Pant were angry on Pannikkar. The then Home Minister G.B. Pant called him 'mischievous'. Pannikkar had served as India's envoy to China with distinction. Even then the then Prime Minister, Nehru 'dropped him like a hot brick'.[10] Charan Singh wanted the bifurcation of Uttar Pradesh, but Morarji Desai, the then Prime Minister of India opposed the proposal. The bifurcation of the same State was announced so casually and in such a hurry by the present Prime Minister without any discussion of any rational parameter. The people of India have accepted 'ad-hocism' as a part of decision-making and have ceased to be angry on the irrational behaviour of their political masters.

REFERENCES

1. *The Hindustan Times*, Patna, November 22, 1995, p. 11.
2. *Ibid.*
3. *Ibid.*
4. *Ibid.*
5. *Ibid.*
6. *Ibid.*
7. *The Hindustan Times*, Patna, *Sunday Magazine*, September 8, 1996, Bobby John Varkey, "States on a Platter"?
8. *Ibid.*
9. *Ibid.*
10. Kuldip Nayar, 'Smaller States Okay, but. . . '; *The Hindustan Times*, Patna, September 1, 1996.

MEETING HALF-WAY

10

THE GORKHALAND IMBROGLIO

THREE subdivisions of Darjeeling district of West Bengal, namely, Darjeeling, Kurseong, and Kalimpong have the total area of 2,200 sq. km. and the population of about seven lakhs. Thus, it has the half of the area and about one-third of the population of an average district of the country. The area is hilly and produces the best tea. Apart from the tea gardens, tourism also provides strong base to the economy of the district.

GORKHALAND

A Sketch Map

MAP 10.1 : Gorkhaland

The demand for the separate State for the area was voiced fifty years ago. The movement was started vigorously by Subhas Ghising on April 13, 1986 for separate Gorkhaland when tempers ran very high in Darjeeling Hill due to the harassment and squeezing out of thousands of Nepalis from the North-East, specially, the Meghalaya. The area was full of the refugees and the number of the takers of Ghising's ideas swelled. Mr. Indra Jit Khullar, a senior journalist and the editor of the

India News and the *Feature Alliance* (INFA) played the role of the 'mysterious' go between. He later on became a Congress (I) Member of the Parliament from Darjeeling Hills with the active support of Ghising. The West Bengal had the Left Front Ministry and the Congress (I) played its own politics, it is alleged, to help Ghising.

The movement was mostly violent one. About 1200 persons were killed and thousands were injured. More than ten thousand houses were set ablazed. The Gorkha National Liberation Front (GNLF) supremo, Subhash Ghising got Darjeeling Gorkha Hill Council on December 26, 1988 as a result of an accord signed between the West Bengal Government, the Centre and the GNLF; Ghising heads the Councils.

Ghising spearheaded the movement for separate Gorkhaland on the plea of the development of Darjeeling Hills. He got the opportunity to develop the area through Darjeeling Gorkha Hill Council. It is most unfortunate that the issue of development was pushed to the background by Ghising himself and he started diverting the attention of the people to non-issues very soon after the formation of the Council. The threat of fresh agitation for separate Gorkhaland State was repeated at regular intervals. This was usually done when the tourist season was about to reach at its peak or at the time of plucking of tea leaves due to the obvious reason. The reason of Ghising's strange behaviour is not difficult to find.

Ghising raised controversy over the status of Nepali language and the Nepalis in India. The DGHC Chairman, Ghising declared Nepali as a foreign language and all Nepalis as foreigners. He demanded the inclusion of Gorkhali, rather than Nepali in the Eighth Schedule of the Constitution. He even threatened to evict Nepalis from Indian soil by force and to launch the agitation for the recognition of Gorkhalis rather than the Nepalis as Indian citizens and Gorkhali language in place of the Nepali.

Ghising advised Nepalis to call themselves Gurkhas to avoid being dubbed as foreigners. What a miraculous prescription? Just change the name and the nationality changes. Such rhetoric, strangely, works with Indian politicians and the journalists. The All India Gorkha League, the Pranta Parishad and the Bhasha Samity formed Samyukta Morcha (United Front) against Ghising and fought for the inclusion of Nepali language in the Eighth Schedule. CPI(M), its leader and the West Bengal Chief Minister, Jyoti Basu and the Sikkim Chief Minister, Nar Bahadur Bhandari worked for the same. Ghising vehemently opposed them. There were demonstrations for and against the move. Ultimately, Nepali language was recognised. The language spoken in Darjeeling is really a dialect of Nepali.

Ghising also raised the bogey of greater Nepal. He quoted Newspaper reports from some papers of Nepal to support his statement. Political circles in West Bengal and Sikkim did not attach much importance to his utterances and Jyoti Basu wrote accordingly to the Union Home Minister, S.B. Chawan. Ghising had strong dislike for Bhandari and wanted to dislodge him from the leadership of the community. It was opined that he aimed at keeping Jyoti Basu on tenterhook and curbing Nar Bahadur Bhandari's influence.[1] Ghising has the 'Igo' problem, it is alleged.[2] According to some sources, he wanted to bring a divide between the higher caste Brahmins and Chetris, the ruling elite of Sikkim, and the backward caste Nepalis, such as the Rais, Limbus, Tamangs and the Gurungs.[3] This card was, of course, played by Mr. Chamling successfully to replace Bhandari later on.

As stated above, the Government of India ignored the plea of Ghising to recognise Gorkhali. Ghising did not take it kindly and threatened to revive the demand for Gorkhaland State and to agitate for the same. He declared:

> "The 1988 Darjeeling accord is dead. And so is the Darjeeling Gorkha Hill Council. I am back to my old path."[4]

Ghising further threatened to boycott the meeting of the National Integration Council in New Delhi on July 18, 1992 in case of the recognition of Nepali.[5]

He further said:

> "Delhi will have to repent for its mistake of recognising Nepali"[6]
> Ghising said that the people of the hills were extremely frustrated over the indifference of the West Bengal Government to the Hill Council and the decision of the Central Government to recognise Nepali.[7] He indirectly threatened by reminding that frustration was the root cause of all movements, like those run by the ULFA, Khalistan and the LTTE.[8]

Nepali Bhasha Samity and Ten Party Front comprising of the Communist Party of India (Marxist), the Akhil Bharatiya Gorkha League, the Gorkha Democratic Front, Communist Party of India, etc. supported the cause of Nepali language. GNLF opposed it. All India Conference on Nepali Language convened by ten party front to be held in Darjeeling on July 11, 1992 was postponed due to the prevailing tension and a 72 hour bandh call with effect from July 10, 1992 by GNLF. It was supposed to be attended by Jyoti Basu and Nar Bahadur Bhandari. The Chief Ministers of Bihar, Uttar Pradesh and Himachal Pradesh (Laloo Prasad Yadav, Kalyan Singh and Shanta Kumar) were invited for the conference.

Ghising termed Nepali speaking people 'reciprocal people' and Nepali, as the language of the 'reciprocal people in terms of reference of the Article 8 of the Indo-Nepalese Treaty, which reads:

> "the Government of India and Nepal agree to grant on reciprocal basis to the nationals of one country in the territories of the other, the same privileges, in the matter of residence, ownership of property, participation in trade and commerce and privileges of a similar matter."

Ghising was the champion of the Nepali language as an active part of an organization, called 'Nilo Jhanda' or Blue Flag Brigade and wrote in a pamphlet, "I was born a Nepali. I will live like a Nepali and I will die a Nepali; even the soil I am to be buried in, will be Nepali."[9] Thus, Ghising's case is unique one. Politics determines everything for him.

Ghising failed to get Gurkhali recognised. Nepali was included in the Eighth Schedule of the Constitution of India. There was no taker for his 'Greater Nepal Conspiracy' theory also. After failing in his above-mentioned game, he invented 'Darjeeling—no Man's Land' theory. This theory has also no taker.

The West Bengal Government raised 57 objections to the activities of the Council in violation of the Hill Council Act related mostly to the disbursement of funds, acquisition of property and appointments.[10] Ghising retaliated. The Chief Executive Officer, L.B. Periyar (a Senior IAS officer, appointed by the West Bengal Government) and the Assistant Executive Officer, Pawan Agarwal, IAS were stripped off their powers and 19 departments of the Council were wounded up after a meeting of the General Council. The Central Committee of the GNLF held a meeting on June 24, 1992 and decided to burn the copies of the Hill Council Act on July 24, 1992. They also decided to send a memorandum to the Prime Minister. Insistence of the Government of West Bengal to follow the rules was viewed as "conspiracy to scuttle the smooth functioning of the Hill Council and render the elected members of the Darjeeling Hill Gorkha Council powerless.[11] The functional and financial indiscipline was equated with smooth functioning and the power of the members with power to break rules. This have become the political *modus operandi* in a large number of cases in our country. Ghising did it openly. They decided to prepare an alternative political solution against the conspiracy mentioned above.[12]

The Panchayat Elections

Holding Village Panchayat election was a constitutional necessity as per the 73rd Amendment to the Constitution (Panchayati Raj Act, 1992). The Panchayat elections were held in West Bengal in April 1994. It could not happen, however, in the Darjeeling Hills due to Ghising's threat of 1,000 hour strike and the fear of revival of the violent agitation. Repeated representations and appeals on behalf of the Government of West Bengal did not bring result.[13]

Ghising was resentful of sharing limited power with the Panchayats, although, he always insisted and demanded more and more power to the Hill Council. He was of the opinion that Panchayat Samitis were parallel administrative structures and elections to these bodies would undermine the autonomy of the Darjeeling Gorkha Hill Council.[14] According to a statement of Ghising, the 'Status' of Darjeeling hills was not clear and it was essential to clear it before the Panchayat elections. The question of holding election did not arise till the status of Darjeeling hills was settled.[15] The Central and the State Governments lacked constitutional and administrative right over the 'disputed territories' of Darjeeling hills till their formal absorption in India according to Ghising.

It may be pointed out that Akhil Bharatiya Gorkha League (ABGL) also demanded early Panchayat Polls. ABGL is the oldest political organization in Darjeeling which became ineffective after the rise of Subhash Ghising and GNLF. It has been revived and has gained its popularity back during the last couple of years.

The Status of Darjeeling

Ghising did not receive support for his theory from the political and academic circles. His mentor and GNLF supported Congress (I) M.P., Inderjit Khullar advised him to move to the Supreme Court. Accordingly, Ghising moved a 25-page writ petition under Article 32 of the Constitution to seek "an appropriate directions from the Supreme Court to the Union Home Ministry for initiating necessary legislative actions under Article 4 read with Article 2 and Article 253 of the Constitution of India for the absorption and formal admission in the Union of India vide

Articles 1(3)(C) of the territories of Kalimpong, the Assam and the Bengal Dooars are acquired as lease-hold territory from Government of Bhutan vide Treaty of Sinchula dated November 11, 1865 as amended by the Treaty of Punakha dated January 8, 1910 and the Indo-Bhutan Treaty of August 8, 1949 as also the territories of Darjeeling which is ceded territory of Nepal vide Treaty of Saquale of 1815, treaty of 1923 and the Indo-Nepal Treaty of 1950."[16]

Darjeeling and the lease-hold land of Kalimpong and Assam and Bengal Dooars were not formally assimilated in India as no Parliamentary legislation referable to Articles 2, 4 and 253 or a constitutional amendment under Article 368 was passed as per the petition. Ghising claimed that the interest of the inhabitants of the area was in jeopardy in the absence of the legislative action and the "ambiguity to the status" of the area had stalled development work.[17] Ghising and the DGHC continued to pass resolutions and write to the appropriate authorities to do the needful in this case.[18] A Division Bench of the Supreme Court dismissed the case on the ground of its being a 'political issue'.[19] Ghising started talking of solving the issue politically after the verdict.

Ghising lives with his confusion shrouded in his ignorance of history. The Ghising phenomenon is based on the selective use of historical material and events on a point of time only. India is a great and vast country with great historical time depth. Ghising has made history a propagandist bundle of confusion, in which only a group of journalists are interested. The conquests and constantly shifting boundaries of the Indian States is a very old historical phenomenon. The history of three very small nucleus of expanding political powers, namely, Nepal, Bhutan and the British in the middle of the eighteenth century is an Indian political phenomena. Nepal and Bhutan were very small principalities and the British were located at the tip of Bengal in a tiny geographical area of Calcutta. All three started expanding at the cost of other Indian States. The conflict situation arose when all three expanding power met. Nepal and British met on the borders of Bihar and Sikkim. British and Bhutan met on the borders of Sikkim, Cooch-Behar and Assam. All three were aggressors. The territories transferred to British India by Nepal and Bhutan did not belong to them. Dooars belonged to Assam and Cooch-Behar and Darjeeling Hills belonged to Sikkim on that point of time.

Mackenzie has written about the 18 dooars. I quote the following paragraphs to show that the territories belonged to India before their annexation/occupation by the Bhutanese:

> "Along the frontier of Bhutan proper lay eighteen of these passes, straths, or dwars, eleven on the frontier of Bengal and Cooch Behar, seven on that of Assam. The land at the foot of the Bengal and Cooch Behar dwars have long since been forcibly annexed by the Bhutias; and the Assamese rulers, though always keenly alive to the value of this malarious Goshen which lay upon their border, and never to the last resigning their claim to be atleast paramount owners of the plains up to the actual mountain ridges, were in their decay unable fully to vindicate their claims. Accordingly, to the hill tribes here, as well as to those on other parts of the border, concessions were made by the Assamese authorities, which it is probable could not have been refused, but which would undoubtedly have been retracted had opportunity made this possible."[19]

Mackenzie has further written about the seven Dooars on the borders of Assam, five in Kamrup (Bijni, Chappakhamar, Chappaguri, Banska and Ghaukola) and two in Darrang (Kalling and Burriguma). Dooars in Goalpara district of Assam were part of Bengal at that time. Mackenzie writes:

> "These seven Dwars, including the tract below them already described, were made over by the Assam Government to Bhutan in consideration of an annual payment of tribute. This tribute was to consist of yak, tails, ponies, musk, gold-dust, blankets and knives, of an estimated value of Naraini Rupees 4,785-1 annually. . . ."[20]

It may not be out of place to quote Edward Gait about the past history of the area, Gait writes:

> ". . . Kamarupa is said to extend from the Karatoya river on the West to the Dikhu on the east, and from the mountain of Kanjagiri on the north, to the confluence of the Brahmaputra and Lakhya rivers on the south; that is to say, it included roughly, the Brahmaputra Valley, Bhutan, Rangapur, Koch Bihar, North-East of Mymensingh and, possible, the Garo Hills."[21]

Gait has quoted *Vishnu Purana*, about the boundary of Assam and further said, ". . . this may be held to embrace the whole of Eastern Bengal, Assam, and Bhutan."[22]

Thus the status of the Dooars as a part of the country is not in dispute. O'Malley has mentioned about the conflict situation between the British and the Nepalese in his '*Gazetteer of Purnea*'.

"The aggression of the Nepalese continued during the next century. In 1908 the Gorkha Governor of the Morung seized the whole zamindari of Bhimnagar. This flagrant encroachment could not be overlooked, and in June, 1809 a detachment of troops was sent to the frontier. The Nepalese, yielding to the threat of an immediate appeal to the sword, evacuated the land next year. In 1814 the first Nepalese war broke out. . . . In 1917, after the conclusion of the war, Major Latter concluded a treaty with the Sikkim Raja at Titalya by which the British granted the latter all the land between the Mechi and the Tista which has been ceded to them by the Nepalese.[23] This part of the land was taken over by the British due to conflict between Sikkim and the British due to the arrest of two British officers, Sir Joseph Hooker and Dr. Campbell in November, 1849."

Darjeeling district was a part of the dominions of the king of Sikkim upto the beginning of the 18th century. Bhutanese took over Kalimpong from them in 1706. This area was acquired by the British after a war with Nepal in 1864.

It may be relevant to point out the fact that Article VIII of the Indo-Nepal Treaty of Peace and Friendship of July 10, 1950 cancels all the clauses of the previous treaties and does not allow and give scope for opening such issues as Ghising is doing. Article VIII reads:

> "The treaty cancels all previous treaties, agreements, and engagements entered into on behalf of India between the British Government and the Government of Nepal."

The Article I of the treaty shows the complete agreement between the two Governments in respect of honouring each other's territorial integrity, etc. and thus the question of disturbing each other's boundaries does not arise. The article reads:

> "The two Governments agree mutually to acknowledge and respect the complete sovereignty, territorial integrity and independence of each other."

The ties of unity were remembered, which provided strong foundation to the treaty. The treaty was signed "recognising the ancient ties which have happily existed between the two countries and desiring still further to strengthen and develop these ties and to perpetuate peace between the two countries.

The questions raised by Ghising undermine the historical truths and the deep foundations of trust and understanding between the people and Government of India and those of its two neighbours are based on foolish assumptions, and are also mischievous. The talk of merger and special status for Darjeeling is a laughable proposition.

As stated earlier, Ghising disliked Bhandari. It is reported that the two have developed tacit understanding after Bhandari lost Gaddi of Sikkim. Bhandari never talked about the merger of Sikkim and Darjeeling till he was Chief Minister of Sikkim. Now, he has realised the need of the same.[24]

Ghising has started voicing the demand for separate Gorkhaland again. Prime Minister, Deve Gowda has given him the chance to do so. He did not rule out the possibility of violence during the struggle for statehood. He said, "I will try my best to avoid bloodshed, but any opposition to the Gorkhaland cause will lead to it."[25] He further said, "A Gorkhaland State is the only alternative."[26]

In the meantime, Deve Gowda's assurance for the creation of Uttarakhand and V.P. Singh's recent support to the reorganization of States have encouraged five national and regional parties to form a joint front—Gorkhaland People's Front (GPF)—to fight for statehood for the Nepali-speaking people in the Darjeeling hills and the neighbouring Jalpaiguri district. The meeting was organised on August 25, 1996 in Darjeeling by the Akhil Bharatiya Gorkha League (ABGL) of Chiten Sherpa, a breakaway group of the GNLF. Madan Tamang, arch rival of Ghising is the President of the new front. Representatives of the Pranta Parishad, the Gorkha Democratic Front (GDF), the Congress (I) and the Bharatiya Janata Party attended the all party meeting. The formation of the Gorkhaland People's Front was welcomed by a large number of organisations, including, the Congress (Tiwari), the Communist Organization India (Marxist-Leninist) or COI (ML), of Kanu Sanyal, Communist Party of India (Marxist-Leninist) of Vinod Mishra and the Minority Forum. It was resolved in all Party meeting that the stir for the statehood would be "united, constitutional, democratic and peaceful."[27] Thus there are two different fora in Darjeeling hills to fight for the statehood now. The decision of the CPI (M) Darjeeling unit to join the statehood movement has demoralised the Communist Party of India (Marxist). Uptil now, they were opposing the move.

It is reported that the Gorkhaland activists have set up camp at Kishanganj in Bihar to enlist the support of the tribal groups and to attempt for the inclusion of parts of Kishanganj and Siliguri thanas in the proposed State.[28] This move may boomerang and create tension in Bihar.

REFERENCES

1. *Sunday*, August 4-10, 1981, p. 18.
2. *Ibid.*
3. *Ibid.*
4. *Frontline*, July 31, 1992, p. 29.
5. *Ibid.*
6. *Ibid.*
7. *Ibid.*
8. *Ibid.*, pp. 29-30.
9. *Ibid.*, p. 30.
10. *Ibid.*
11. *Ibid.*
12. *Ibid.*
13. *Frontline*, December 30, 1994, p. 37.
14. *The Hindustan Times*, Patna, Editorial, 'Call his Bluff'; September 5, 1995.
15. *Frontline*, op. cit., p. 37.
16. *Ibid.*, p. 37-38.
17. *Ibid.*, p. 38.
18. *Ibid.*
19. Mackenzie, A., *History of the Relation of the Government with the Hill Tribes of the North East Frontier of Bengal*, p. 9.
20. *Ibid.*, p. 10.
21. Gait, Edward, *A History of Assam*, p. 10. Quotes the opinion of Yogini Tantra.
22. *Ibid.*
23. Roy Choudhury, P.C., *Bihar District Gazetteer*, Purnia, pp. 87-88.
24. *Frontline*, December 30, 1994, p. 38.
25. *Ibid.*, October 4, 1996, p. 43.
26. *Ibid.*
27. *Ibid.*
28. *The Hindustan Times*, Patna, dated October 8, 1996.

11

UNENDING CONFLICT IN BODOLAND

THE Bodos are one of the most important tribes of North-East India. A large number of languages of the region, including Garo of Meghalaya, Tripuri (Kok-Borok) of Tripura and Dimasa Cachari of the North Cachar Hills have linguistic affinity with the Bodo language. They are closely allied to the Koches, the Chutiyas, the Lalungs and the Morans of the Brahmaputra Valley. Tantric Hinduism, Shaktism and Shaivism had great hold over the community. Vaishnava Movements of the great teachers of Assam, Shri Shankar Deva and Shri Madhav Deva had large followers among the community. They worship Lord Shiva and call him Bathow. The Brahma religious movement was a Hindu Reform movement started by Gurudeva Kalicharan Brahma (earlier name, Kalicharan Mech). The contribution of the Bodos in giving the present shape to the culture, society and religion of North-East India, specially, the Assam is great.

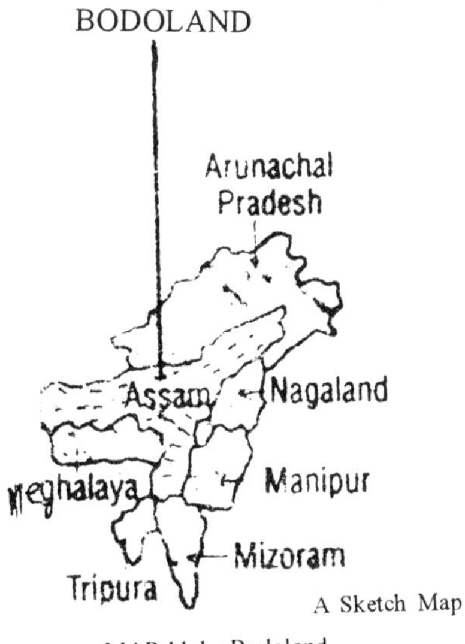

MAP 11.1 : Bodoland

Edward Gait was a colonial historian. He wrote *A History of Assam* with colonial mentality. Gait found Bodo root 'di' or 'ti' (water) in the names of the rivers of Assam and gave a strange twist to the history of Assam.[1] Gait should have tried to search the word for water in some other non-Bodo languages. The word 'Toya' of the Sanskrit, and 'Tui' of Mizo are two of the many examples. The diverse ethnic groups lived in Assam in perfect harmony for thousands of years. The seeds of discord and mistrust was sown by the mischievous colonial historians. The hypothesis to declare Bodos as the earliest settlers on the basis of faulty presumptions was a colonial mischief.

The demands of small States in India defies all logic. The economic viability, reasonable size and population, etc. ceases to be the valid criteria for the formation of a State. The only valid criterion for the Statehood demand during the last three decades was the assertion of separate ethnic identity. This resulted into the arrest of the process of social and cultural assimilation and that of 'give and take' going on for centuries in this part of the country. The process of social distancing was deliberately started by many communities, such as, the Bodos from the Assamese.

The effectiveness of agitations, bundhs, disruptions in public life, economic blocades and violence as means of securing autonomy and statehood resulted in weakening of the fabrics of the society and the establishments of the cult of gun, nay, that of the machine guns and AK 47s. This made the society coward and robbed it of its sensitivities. The murders do not shock the people now. The effectiveness of the cult of gun and social disruption for securing autonomy was intensively tested in the North-East. The technique is being used elsewhere now. Gorkhaland agitation was by and large violent. The violence has shown its face in Jharkhand also. The wrong signals were, somehow, sent knowingly or unknowingly that the violence pays, and there are many takers of the same.

The widely circulated stories of the scams, Hawala, LOCs, defalcations, mis-appropriations of public funds, etc. has exposed the real character of our political elite. This is a countrywide phenomenon. However, the continued heaviest reliance on the Consolidated Fund of India for running the State is mostly a characteristic of some of the small States. The example is not lacking where a State collects only 10 per cent of the revenue and gets 90 per cent from the Consolidated Fund of India. This is classic example of getting power without responsibility; bread without labour. Ironically, such States have created permanent unnecessary burden due to over-employment. Some States have developed vested interest in backwardness. The insurgency and intense violent activities helped them, as these diverted the attention of others from the failures of the State Governments. The quantum of per capita central assistance, in some cases, was directly proportional to the intensity of the deviant Constitutional demands. Needless to say that this phenomenon did not go unnoticed and there were many takers.

The Bodos were not immune to the developments in the North-East. They witnessed the formation of tribal States in North-East with lesser population than that of the Bodos. However, the Bodos had a serious difficulty. Unlike other tribal communities enjoying the benefits of Statehood, such as, the Nagas, the Mizos, the Khasis and the Garos, they did not have a compact area of their own. They did not constitute majority population in any district of Assam. The Bodo population in various districts of Assam according to 1971 census is given below:[1]

District	*Total Population*	*Number of the Bodo speaking persons*	*Percentage of the total population*
Assam	1,46,25,162	5,33,713	3.65
Goalpara	22,25,103	2,32,537	10.45
Kamrup	28,54,183	1,39,761	4.90
Darrang	17,36,188	97,829	5.63
Nagaon	16,80,895	8,511	0.31
Sibsagar	18,37,389	2,013	0.11
Dibrugarh	14,11,119	36	—
Lakhimpur	7,11,600	18,207	2.56
Karbi Anglong	3,79,310	28,265	7.45
North Cachar Hills	76,047	4,993	6.57
Cachar	17,13,318	1561	0.09

The slogan of the protagonists of Bodoland Movement is "Divide Assam 50/50." But, how? Where is the Bodo majority area in Assam? True, there are Bodo majority pockets. But again, such areas are not contiguous. All the previous logic fails here. There is demand for an ethnic State without ethnic majority. But the same process was in operation in Jharkhand movement also. It was basically a demand for a tribal State with tribal majority only in three districts of the area claimed. Of course, Jharkhand is a regional demand now. Moreover, logic is the first casualty in the process of the demand for autonomy and State in North-East India, where a very small community like Tiya of Assam and Hmar of Mizoram may also claim and agitate for autonomy and succeed in their efforts.

Two points, which are specific in the case of the Bodoland State demand need mention. Firstly, it was the first demand, as stated above, where a State was demanded by a community without having a compact area of their own and without their majority in the area. Secondly, organized attacks by armed insurgent groups on the Muslim and Santal villagers took the shape of attempt towards ethnic purge to secure higher percentage of population and hegemony. I shall discuss this aspect in this chapter afterwards.

The Bodos started the demand for autonomous State very late almost in the mid-1980s. However, there were many attempts to project the needs of the community in the past. Gurudev Kalicharan Brahma represented before the Simon Commission that the seats in the Legislative Assembly and the Government jobs should be reserved for the tribals. The Tribal League was formed in Assam in 1930 to focus the attention on the political and socio-economic problems of the tribals. He supported the league in its activities. The Tribal League was transformed into a socio-cultural organization called Tribal Sangh after independence. The Bodo Sahitya Sabha was established in 1952, which spearheaded the Bodo script movement later on. Devanagari script was accepted in place of Assamese as a result of that movement. Their attempt resulted into the acceptance of Bodo language as the medium of instruction in the primary and later on in secondary schools of the Bodo majority areas of Assam.

Growth of Political Organizations

The Plains Tribal Council of Assam (PTCA) was the first political organization of the Bodos. It was formed at Kokrajhar on February 27, 1967 under the chairmanship of Modoram Brahma. The All Bodo Students' Union was formed later on in the 1970s. The ABSU played vital role in the political life of the Bodos later on.

The tribal leaders from the plains of Assam were encouraged by the Government's announcement to give federal form to the State of Assam. They were inspired by that development and formed PTCA. Although PTCA was the party of all the plains tribals of Assam, nevertheless there was Bodo domination in the Party. The Party gave a call for the boycott of 1967 Parliament election and 1968 bye-elections from Kokrajhar. It submitted a memorandum to the Prime Minister, Shrimati Indira Gandhi for the creation of the autonomous region called 'Udayachal' in November 1972. The PTCA launched a movement on December 7, 1973 for the formation of Union Territory, called Udayachal. The PTCA and ABSU supported Bodo Sahitya Sabha led movement for the recognition of Roman script for the Bodo language. Ultimately, Devanagari script was accepted by them. The PTCA fought Parliament and Assembly elections, won many seats and continued to petition for Udayachal. The Party ultimately became ineffective in 1985 due to frequent shift of their allegiance from one party to another and the sudden withdrawal of their demand for a Union Territory in favour of earlier demand for Autonomous Region. There was split in the Party. The deserters formed PTCA(P) and demanded the formation of an Union Territory, called Mishing Bodoland. The leadership of the autonomy movement shifted in the hands of All Bodo Students' Union in 1986. The students were inspired by the success of All Assam Students Union and their *modus operandi* and followed their technique in running the movement. The movement was non-violent in the beginning, but turned out violent within a short time.

The Union Territory demand was upgraded to that of the full-fledged Bodoland State demand in the twentieth annual conference of the ABSU held at Bashbari in Dhubri district on December 19-22, 1988. The militant phase of the movement started just after that. There was enormous increase in the terrorist activity in the State during that period. All Bodo Students' Union—Bodo People's Action Committee (ABSU-BPAC) stepped up their activities. There was frequent disruption in public life due to frequent *bundhs*, violent acts, etc.

There were two rounds of talks between the State Government and ABSU. The talks did not bear fruit. The ABSU declined the offer of the State Government for another round of talks to be held in February, 1989. A series of talks between the representatives of the Central and the State Governments and the ABSU followed without any tangible result. It was decided to form a three-member Expert Committee at the extended session of the eighth round of talks. The Expert Committee was to recommend on the autonomy, the administration, the legislative and the financial powers to be granted to the Bodos. The Expert Committee submitted its report in March 1992 and suggested to give maximum autonomy to the Bodos under the State of Assam. The Bodo leaders rejected the recommendations. The movement continued.

The Bodos wanted the inclusion of 4443 villages under the proposed unit spread over nine districts. A meeting of the Bodo leaders was held with the representatives of the State Government, in which the Bodos wanted the inclusion of another 209 villages with tribal population and 1035 without the tribal population. This led to breakdown of the talks.

The State Government wanted the Central Government to intervene. The tripartite discussions, in which Rajesh Pilot participated finally brought fruit. The Memorandum of Understanding (popularly known as Bodoland Accord) was signed on February 21, 1993. The Bodoland Autonomous Council (BAC) was created with 2000 villages and 25 Tea Gardens in its area. The area between the river Sankosh and river Pasnoi/Majbat on the north bank of the river Brahmaputra have the villages with more than 50 per cent tribal population. However, a large number of villages with less than 50 per cent tribal population are also included to maintain the contiguity.

The Bodoland Autonomous Council Bill was introduced in the Assam Assembly on April 5, 1993. The BAC Act was subsequently passed. There is a provision of a General Council consisting of 40 members. The council's general body shall have 35 elected and five nominated members. There are 25 reserved seats for the Plains Tribals and ten are general seats. An Indian citizen, not below the age of 18 years and not holding any position in any Municipality or Panchayat or any office of the Central and the State Government is eligible to be a candidate for election for the General Council of the BAC. The term of office of a member is for five years. The Governor may extend the term for a period not exceeding one year if it becomes impossible to hold the election in time. The Governor has the power to remove an elected member, if he is found to be dishonest.

The General Council shall meet atleast once in three months. The quorum is formed by thirteen members and the decision is taken by the single majority vote of the members present. Thirty-eight subjects, including, Education, Panchayat and Rural Development, PHE, Transport, Tourism, Forest, Agriculture, PWD, Tribal Welfare, etc. come under the jurisdiction of the Council. The full list is given in the Annexure-4.

The General Council will be responsible for the formulation and implementation of the development programmes within its area. It has the power to appoint class III and class IV employees, regulate trade and commercial activities including the power to issue permits and licenses to individuals; to organise special recruitment drive into army, para-military forces and police units, etc., where preference will be given to the Bodos.

The General Council will manage its finances and raise finances from levies, fees, taxes, etc. on subjects under their jurisdiction. The finances for the BAC area will be earmarked under a separate sub-head within the State budget. The revenue collected by the Assam Government from the BAC area will be deposited in the BAC Fund.

The Council will have power to formulate by-laws for implementation within its territory. It must be consulted in case of any new law to be introduced under any circumstances in the BAC area on the following subjects:

(i) The religious or the social practices of the Bodos;
(ii) The Bodo Customary Laws and Procedures; and
(iii) The ownership and transfer of land within the Council's area.

The Council has the power to make bye-laws, but the power of the State legislature is over-riding. The Clause 54 of the bill says:

> "If any provision of any regulation and bye-law made by the General Council is repugnant to any provision of a law made by the Legislature of the State of Assam with respect to that matter, then, the regulation or bye-law so made by the Bodoland Council, shall to the extent of the repugnancy, be void and the law made by the Legislature of the State of Assam shall prevail."

There is provision for the promotion of the Bodo language. The bill provides for setting up of special courts—Village Courts, Subordinate District Customary Law Courts, and District Customary Law Courts in consultation with the Guwahati High Court to try the cases according to the customary laws if all the parties belong to the tribal communities.

The BAC will have Executive Council (Bodoland Executive Council or BEC) with a Chief, a Deputy Chief and seven members elected from among the members of the BAC. The Chairman and the Vice-Chairman of the BAC shall become the Chief and the Deputy Chief of BEC at the time of the first sitting of BAC.

The executive functions of the General Council vests in the Bodoland Executive Council. The General Council and the Bodoland Executive Council will hold office during the pleasure of the Governor of Assam, and if the situation compels, then the Governor has the supreme power to dissolve either the General Council or the BEC, by a notification, even prior to the expiry of its actual term. Under such circumstances the authorised persons (authorised by the Governor) would hold responsibility to run the administration.

As per the provision of the BAC, the decision of the State Government on interpretation of any of the provisions of the Act or rules thereunder will be final. Only the State Government is empowered to remove any kind of confusion that may arise in regard to the implementation of the Act.

The Bodoland Accord provides for the change of the geographical boundary of the BAC area (as per Clause 12 of the Accord) with the mutual consent of the BAC members and the Government of Assam. This is one of the reasons that the BAC continues to demand the inclusion of 515 villages in the BAC area.[2]

There is provision for the Constitution of an 'Interim Bodoland Executive Council of the BAC'. It was to be constituted from amongst the leaders of the movement till the elections are held. It may be mentioned that the elections were to be held within six months only after the Constitution of the Interim Council, but the Government of Assam failed to arrange timely election of BAC.

Inclusion of Non-Bodo Villages in the BAC Area

The Bodoland accord did not give equal status to all the tribal communities residing in the notified area. This evoked criticism and even active protest from some of the communities. The Adivasis Council of Assam resented non-inclusion of Adivasis in the list of the Scheduled Tribes. The Central Committee of the Adivasi Council issued a press-release, which said:[3]

> "Both the Government and the ABSU leaders have failed to include the Adivasis like Santhals, Mundas, Oraons, Gonds, Bheels, etc. in the Scheduled Tribe list in spite of the fact that both Government and the ABSU leaders have supported their demands."

The leaders of the Koch Rajbongshi community were apprehensive about their future and the denial of equal political status to their community.[4] Needless to say that there was serious reaction among the Koch-Rajbongshi community against the accord and the All Assam Koch-Rajbongshi Kshatriya Sanmilani decided to stage a *dharna* on March 16, 1993 in front of Janata Bhawan in Guwahati to demand for the right of their self-determination. Shri Phani Medhi, President of the Sanmilani announced to the news-men:[5]

> "the proposed Bodo Autonomous Council area would include a population of 18 lakh people of whom 12 lakh belong to Koch-Rajbongshi community. . . . while signing the memorandum none of the signatories paid any heed to the aspirations of the section of the people and their fate has been placed at the mercy of the Bodo leaders, in the name of the geographical contiguity of the BAC area. . . ."

As already stated, a large number of such villages were included in the notified area of the Bodoland Autonomous Council which had either less than 50 per cent Bodo population or no Bodo population at all. There were reports about the forcible eviction of non-tribals from some of the villages. The statement of Shri Nagen Sarma of the Assam Gana Parishad in a Press meet is given below:[6]

> "Villages with less than 50 per cent tribal population and even some villages with no tribal population were included in the Council area. He alleged that though the Chief Minister had assured that steps would be taken for safeguarding the rights of the non-tribals living in the Council area, the Bodo people were evicting non-tribals from some of the villages proposed to be included in the Council area."

Inclusion of the Tea Gardens in the BAC Area

The inclusion of 25 Tea Gardens in the BAC area was resented by many persons and organizations, including Shri Prafulla Kumar Mahanta, former Chief Minister, Shashkamal Handique of CPI(M), INTUC and the Assam Chah Mazdur Sangh (ACMS). The ACMS warned the Assam Government against the inclusion of the Tea Gardens and said that the future of about 35,000 garden workers would be in jeopardy under the new administration set-up.[7]

The Reaction of the Bodos

The Bodos by and large welcomed the accord. However, there was opposition of the same from a section of the community also. A section of the Bodos were not happy with the accord due to non-inclusion of the Bodo areas of the Sonitpur, Dhemaji and Lakhimpur districts.[8] The Bodos of the south bank of Brahmaputra were not happy due to the same reason.[9]

The Bodo Security Force (an outlawed militant organization) continued to indulge in violent activities and oppose the accord as the avowed aim of the organization is separation from India. They are also asking for the adoption of Roman script for the Bodo language.

Soft State Syndrome and the Armed Activities of BAC Area

It is reported that the Bodo Security Force militants are imparting arms training to recruits near Daifam in Bhutan and Arunachal Pradesh jungles. It was reported that ". . . more than 3,000 youth were being groomed for guerrilla warfare like ambushes and the like. Meanwhile, sophisticated weapons like carbines and stenguns in large numbers, about 1000 AK 47 rifles, a good number of LMGs, 2-3 inch mortars and large quantities of bottle bombs, etc. were being piled up by the BdSF militants."[10]

It is pertinent to mention here that two important factors, apart from some minor factors are responsible for the genesis and growth of organizations like BdSF in North-East India. I shall discuss them in brief.

(i) The Government continues to ignore the genuine grievances of the people, which often causes frustration, anger and alienation. The development machinery of the Government has failed to deliver the desired good to the poor people of this country. At the same time, it has worked for enormous rise in the expectations of the people from the Government. The gap between what is expected and what they get is unbridgeable. This prepares suitable ground for the trouble-shooters. Another factor, which has brought alienation is the unabated flow of the Bangladeshi immigrants. The Muslim immigrants started coming to Assam after 1905, when Assam was tugged with East Bengal in 1905. They occupied the forest reserves, waste lands and *char* (i.e., Diara) lands. The famous line system was introduced in 1920 in Barpeta subdivision of Kamrup district (Now, Barpeta district) and Nowgong district to prevent the immigrants from settling in the 40 blocks, where tribals alone were supposed to have land. In spite of the safeguards, the Muslim settlement continued in those blocks. The immigrants also acquired land by fraud or force in that area. Today, there are 70 per cent landless tribal labourers in the area within the said line. The Barpeta massacre took place in the same area couple of years ago. The immigration of the illegal Bangladeshis is yet to stop in that area and of course in the rest of the country. This angers the people enormously. The Government should rise above the vote-bank politics and see that the genuine concerns of the people are not overlooked.

Sometimes, the provocation comes from the unexpected corner and the Government fails to act. This is why, "despite the promises of the State Government that none of the culprits would go scot-free, MPs like Mr. G.G. Swell have wanted to know subsequently why no action have been taken against a minister who had led an attack on a Bodo village and openly incited mobs to retaliate."[11]

(ii) The keen observers of North-East may realise that the underground militant outfits in North-East India do not grow overnight and hit back. Such organizations take years to grow and the matter is known to the Central and State Governments through the intelligence agencies, who send their reports regularly. The growth of such organizations is not checked at the infant stage due to negligence, apathy and soft State Syndrome of the Central and State Governments. If Government takes appropriate action at appropriate time then organizations like BDSF, ULFA and NSCN may not grow strong roots.

The Policy Lapses and the Attempts of Ethnic Purge

The Bodoland is a classic example of lack of policy and ad-hocism in tackling the ethnic problems. The Bodos are a minority group in the BAC area, and yet, they have been given the power to control the majority population of their area without the consent of the latter. The recent attempt to attack and massacre unarmed Santhal villagers and the attack on the minority villages by Bodo militants seem to be an attempt towards manipulating a majority for the Bodos in the BAC area. Such trend must be arrested. So far the Muslim population in the BAC area is concerned, no Indian Muslim should be harmed at any cost. At the same time, no illegal immigrant should be allowed to stay in BAC area or anywhere in India. The attempt to mix the identity of Indian and Bangladeshi Muslims should not succeed at any cost. The speedier deportation of the Bangladeshi may ease the tension in Bodo inhabited area to a large extent.

Adequate legal provision to safeguard the interests of the Koch-Rajbongshis, Adivasis, and the other communities of the BAC area should be made without any further delay.

Failures, Internal Strife, Fratricidal War and the Attempts of Reconciliation

It was three and half years ago in 1993 that Bodoland Autonomous Council was formed. The demand for inclusion of a 10 km. stretch of land to the BAC area was made at that time. It was also expected that the election for the permanent Council should take place within six months of the formation of the interim Council. The demand for the election was repeatedly made. Both these demands remained unfulfilled uptil now. It is widely admitted that the development work during the three years period of the Interim Council under the Chiefship of Prem Singh Brahma was insignificant. The usual complaint as voiced by Bineshwar Brahma, President, Bodo Sahitya Sabha that "everything had to be sanctioned by the State Government. This was no autonomy,"[12] also justified the 'no performance' status of the Interim Council.

The All Bodo Students Union demanded the inclusion of 10 km area along the international border in the BAC area. The demand was not met. This sparked off a spate of violent killings. The new political parties were formed, namely, the Bodoland Statehood Movement Council (BSMC) and the People's Democratic Front (PDF), just after the violent incidents. These parties took part in the last Assembly elections. The PDF won six seats and the BSMC two. AGP formed Government with the outside support of PDF.[13] Prem Singh Brahma was deposed soon after. Kanakeshwar Narzari was made the Chief Executive Member of the Bodoland Autonomous Council soon after the new government was installed in the State.[14]

The peace continues to elude the area. The All Bodo Students Union President, M.S. Bwismutiary was gunned down in Kokrajhar sometime back. It is suspected that the killing is done by Bodo Security Force.

A convention of all the political parties was called by the Bodo Sahitya Sabha on August 17 and 18, 1996. The Bodo National Peace and Coordination Committee was formed in that meeting. Bineshwar Brahma is the President of the new organization. He has clearly stated the objective of the organization:

"Stopping the fratricidal killing is of the utmost priority. It is more important than the demand for a separate State."[15]

REFERENCES

1. The Census of India, Series 3, Assam Part I-A, 1971, p. 91.
2. *The Hindustan Times*, May 7, 1995, p. 6. K. Khogen Singh, 'Bodos Still Chasing an Illusive Autonomy'.
3. *The Assam Tribune*, March 14, 1993.
4. *The Shillong Times*, March 10, 1993.
5. *The Assam Tribune*, March 5, 1993.
6. *Ibid.*, February 25, 1993.
7. *The Shillong Times*, March 10, 1993.
8. *The North East Times*, March 2, 1993.
9. *Sadin* (Assamese) June 18, 1993.
10. *The Tribune*, March 18, 1993.
11. *The Sentinel*, July 29, 1994, Editorial, 'Mr. Pilot On Barpeta'.
12. *India Today*, October 15, 1996, p. 87.
13. *Ibid.*
14. *Ibid.*
15. *Ibid.*

12

THE JHARKHAND MOVEMENT AND THE JAAC

THE demand for the Jharkhand State is one of the oldest in this country. The attempt to organise the people of the region was made in 1916, when a group of Christian tribals formed the Chota Nagpur Improvement Society to work for the preservation of their identity. Unnati Samaj, the political wing of the Christian Tribals' Association submitted the memorandum to the Simon Commission to constitute a tribal State in the Eastern India in 1928. The Adivasi Mahasabha defined the boundary of Jharkhand in 1939. The Mahasabha got itself registered as 'Jharkhand Party' in due course. Jaipal Singh, a Christian Munda tribal leader, was the main architect of the Party.

The details of the areas claimed and the population of the Jharkhand State is given below:[1]

State	*Districts*	*Area*	*Population*
Bihar	18 districts (Deoghar, Godda, Sahibganj, Pakur, Dumka, Dhanbad, Bokaro, Hazaribagh, Koderma, Giridih, Chatra, Palamu, Garhwa, Ranchi, Gumla, Lohardaga, Purbi Singhbhum, Pashchimi Singhbhum)	80,334.6	2,32,98,740
Madhya Pradesh	Surguja, Raigarh	35,261	38,07,350
West Bengal	Bankura, Midnapore	20,963	1,11,49,345
Orissa	Sundargarh, Sambalpur, Tharsuguda, Deogada, Mayurbhanja, Keonjhar	40,283	62,40,630
	Total	1,76,841.6	4,44,96,065

The area is very rich in the mineral wealth and more than 50 per cent of the minerals of the country is concentrated in this region.

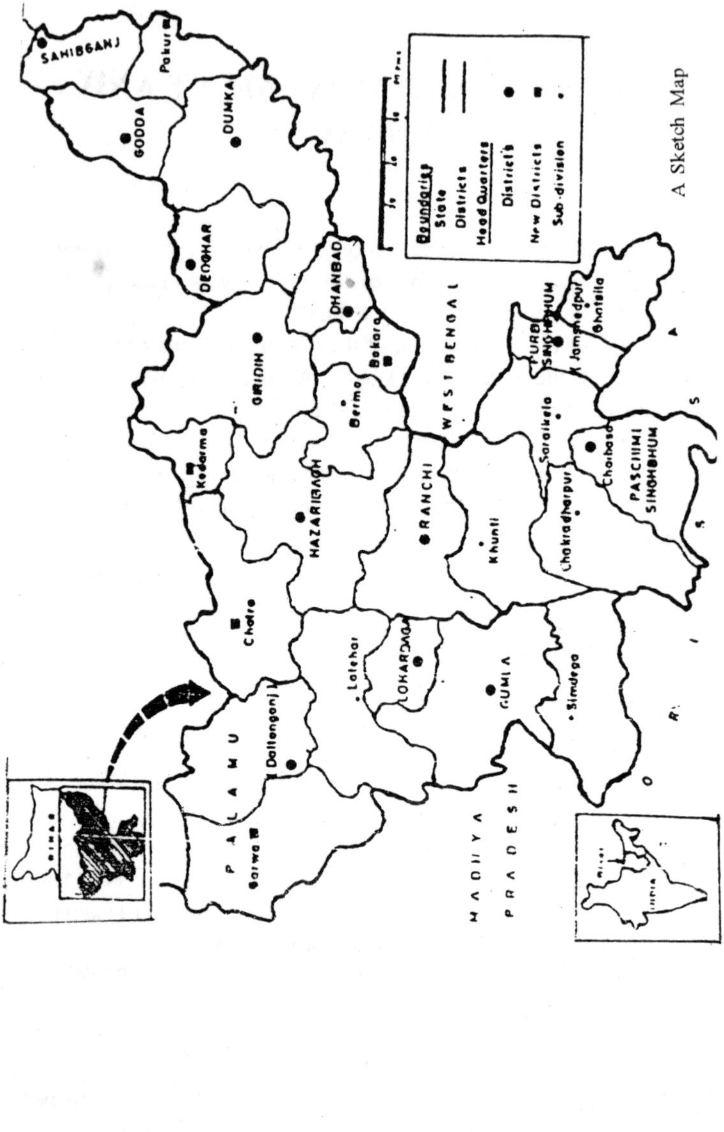

A Sketch Map

MAP 12.1 : Jharkhand Autonomous Area

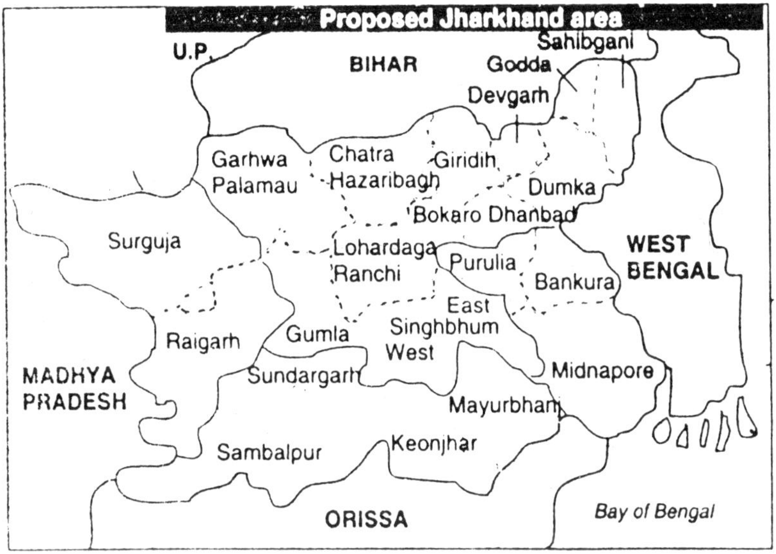

A Sketch Map

MAP 12.2 : Proposed Jharkhand Area

The region was known by various names in the past, such as, Dasharn, Kikat and Jharkhand. There were two Dasharns. One was near Bhopal. Dasharn means 'Ten Forts'. The word Jharkhand was in use in the olden days and also during the Mughal days. The British formed South West Frontier Agency with headquarters at Hazaribagh in 1833 clubbing the tribal areas of that region. Santal Pargana was made a separate district after the Santal rebellion in 1855 and declared a non-regulation district area under Regulation XXXVII of 1855. The Chota Nagpur was already under separate administration after the Kol Mutiny of 1831. It may be mentioned that the area witnessed many revolts against the British, such as the Ho revolt (1820), Kol Mutiny (1831), Santal Rebellion (1855), and the Birsa Movement (1900). The Santal Pargana and the Chota Nagpur were covered under the provisions of the Scheduled District Act (Act XIV) of 1874 as scheduled districts. Many other acts were passed at different times by the British government keeping the needs of the area in mind, such as, the Chota Nagpur Tenancy Encumbered Estates Act, 1876; the Chota Nagpur Commutation Act (Act II of 1897), Chota Nagpur Tenancy (Amendment) Act of 1903 and the Chota Nagpur Tenancy Act of 1903.

Some of the characteristics of Jharkhand Movement in its early days are given below:

(i) It was mostly a tribal movement. Anti-Diku sentiments found open expressions in their meetings. Diku and Sadan are the common words for the Non-Tribals in this region.
(ii) The Christian dominance was the accepted fact.
(iii) The leaders, mostly, belonged to the Munda and Oraon communities.
(iv) It has urban leanings.
(v) Discrimination against the non-tribals on the name of tribal unity created deep-rooted distrust between the tribals and the Sadans.

There was a slow gradual change in the above-mentioned characteristics of the movement. Jharkhand Party changed from an Ethnic Party to a Regional Party. The Santal leaders, such as, Sibu Soren became more prominent in the movement. The participation of the non-Christians increased. The area of influence and activity decreased mostly to parts of Bihar and Orissa.

Most of the writers and the protagonists of Jharkhand put too much emphasis on the tribal aspect of Jharkhand. It creates Tribe-Sadan divide in Chhota Nagpur. The same mentality is seen in Bodo inhabited area of Assam. The mentality has brought deep-rooted Bodo-Non-Bodo divide there. It may be mentioned that tribal population in Jharkhand region of Bihar is only 28 per cent of the total population of the region. The tribals form majority in three districts of Gumla (71%), Lohardaga (56%) and Pashchim Singhbhum (55%). The tribal population in some other districts are Dhanbad (8%), Hazaribagh (9%), Giridih (12%), Deoghar (13%) and Palamu (18%).

Jharkhand Party actively participated in the general election of 1952. The Party won 33 seats in the Bihar Legislative Assembly and three seats in the Parliament from Bihar alone. The popularity of the party declined sharply and it could win only 20 seats in Bihar Legislative Assembly in 1962 elections. This highly discouraged Jaipal Singh. The people also favoured Congress due to the industrialization of the region during the first-two plans.

The Jharkhand Party submitted memorandum to the States' Reorganization Commission for the creation of Jharkhand State. Their demand was, however, not conceded due to the following reasons:

(i) Linguistic plurality and the absence of a link language,
(ii) Lack of Tribal majority, and
(iii) The adverse effect on the economy of the State after separation of the Jharkhand area.

Jaipal Singh was highly disappointed due to declining popularity of his party and the rejection of the State demand by the SRC. He merged his party with the Congress Party in 1963. However, entire rank and file of the party did not join the Congress. Sushil Kumar Bage, N.E. Horo and Bugun Sumbrui brought split in the party and revived the Jharkhand Party again. Factions led by N.E. Horo and Bugun Sumbrui separated again causing further split. 'Ahul Jharkhand' Party was formed by Justice Richard in 1968. Sibu Soren formed Jharkhand Mukti Morcha in 1973. It won seven seats in 1980 Assembly elections. Jharkhand Mukti Morcha (JMM) also could not remain united and split into Jharkhand Mukti Morcha (Soren) and Jharkhand Mukti Morcha (Mardi).

JMM(S) was instrumental in the formation of All Jharkhand Students Union (AJSU). The AJSU intensified Jharkhand Movement again in late 1980s. AJSU introduced the element of violence in the Jharkhand politics. The JMM(S) opposed the poll boycott call given by AJSU during 1990 Assembly polls, which resulted into the parting of ways between the two organizations.

The efforts towards the unity between various Jharkhand outfits resulted into the formation of Jharkhand Coordination Committee (JCC). The JCC could not become an effective organization due to prevailing differences between various parties.

The efforts to renew Jharkhand demand were made from time to time. N.E. Horo, leader of the Jharkhand Party sent a memorandum to the Prime Minister in 1973. In his memorandum, Horo countered the objections raised by the SRC against the statehood demands.

There was provision for limited internal autonomy for the hill districts of Assam under the Sixth Schedule of the Constitution of India. Other hill/tribal areas were covered by the Fifth Schedule of the Constitution. The Chhota Nagpur and Santal Pargana Development Board was constituted under the Chairmanship of the Chief Minister of Bihar in 1972 under the provisions of the Fifth Schedule. Kartick

Oraon, veteran tribal leader was the Vice-Chairman of the Board. Rs. 3 crores was sanctioned for the development work through the board. The board failed to achieve the desired result and to satisfy the people.

The Jharkhand Coordination Committee was led by Dr. Ram Dayal Munda, Ex-Vice-Chancellor of Ranchi University; Dr. B.P. Keshari, B.B. Mahato, Santosh Rana and Suraj Singh Besra. The JCC started fresh initiatives in the Jharkhand affairs. B.P. Keshari sent memorandum for the formation of Jharkhand State. Their efforts continued for solving Jharkhand tangle.

Committee on Jharkhand Matters (COJM)

The Central Government formed a Committee on Jharkhand Matters in 1989.[1] The 24-member high power Committee has experts on 'Tribal Development' like, Dr. Bhupendra Singh and Dr. Kumar Suresh Singh. The Committee submitted its report for the formation of a 'Jharkhand Area Council' (JAC), which was presented in the Parliament on March 30, 1992. The Committee suggested that the election of the 50 members of the JAC should be done by an electoral group consisting of the Chairmen and the members of the Village Panchayats and District Boards. There should be an Executive Committee consisting of 11 members. They also suggested that an Advisory Committee consisting of the MPs, MLAs and the members of the JAC should also be formed.

The Committee stressed the need of greater allocation of the development funds for the area. It said in its report:

> "The Jharkhand region contributes about 70 per cent of the revenue to the State exchequer, in return, it receives only 30 per cent for utilisation. It should receive in proportion to the respective accruals."

The report emphasised the need of speedier economic development, autonomy in economic, legal and administrative matters, responsible and helpful bureaucracy, progressive cultural policy, etc.

One day Jharkhand Bandh was organised on September 15, 1992. The Jharkhand Peoples Party and the All Jharkhand Students Union jointly organised 15 days' Economic Blocade. The Union Home Minister, S.B. Chawan's statement in September from Shillong hinted at the possibility of the separation of Jharkhand as a State or Union Territory. It generated heat and tension. Both Laloo Prasad Yadav, the Chief Minister of Bihar and Jagannath Mishra opposed it. A compromise formula gradually evolved basing on the recommendations of the COJM. As a result, the Jharkhand Area Autonomous Council was born.

Jharkhand Area Autonomous Council

An agreement was signed in New Delhi on September 20, 1994 by Laloo Prasad Yadav, the Chief Minister of Bihar, Rajesh Pilot, Union Minister of State for Internal Security and JMM leaders, Sibu Soren and Suraj Mandal in the presence of the Prime Minister, P.V. Narasimha Rao to form the JAAC. The JAAC bill was placed in Bihar Legislative Assembly in December 1994 and passed. An earlier Bill, passed by both the Houses of the Legislature in 1972 for the Constitution of Jharkhand Autonomous Development Council, and sent for the assent of the President was withdrawn.[2]

There was split in JMM on the issue of withdrawal of JMM support from Laloo Prasad Yadav Government[3] and giving Rajya Sabha seat to Subodh Kant Sahay.[4] Krishna Mardi faction separated with nine MLAs and formed JMM (M). JMM (M) started supporting Laloo government. However, there was very soon the reversal of roles. JMM (S) became pro-Laloo and JMM (M) against him. The JMM (M) opposed the idea of JAAC and JMM (S) supported the same. The JAAC was constituted with Sibu Soren, President, JMM (S) as its Chairman.

The BJP and the Jharkhand Party opposed the formation of JAAC. The Jharkhand People's Party and Chhotanagpur Santal Pargana Regional Congress (I) Committee (CSPRCC-I) wanted more powers for the Council. Bharatiya Janata Party opposed the Council due to its demand of Vananchal State. Eventually, JMM (S) and the Janata Dal were the only parties, which favoured the formation of the new Council. AJSU-JPP combine went to the extent of declaring their intention to launch struggle to ensure that greater powers were vested in the proposed Jharkhand Area Autonomous Council.[5]

Jharkhand Area Autonomous Council was formed on August 9, 1995. An interim Council, consisting of 90 members was formed. Out of 90 members 41 belonged to JMM (S), 31 from the Janata Dal and remaining from the other parties. An atmosphere of resentment prevailed. The post of Vice-Chairman went to Suraj Mandal, M.P. for which JMM (M), AJSU and the JPP vied with each other. All the major political parties, including the Jharkhand Parties criticised its formation. The BJP, the Congress (I), the Jharkhand Party (Horo), the JMM (Mardi), and even, Shailendra Mahato, M.P. and Sudhir Mahato of JMM (S) boycotted it. The latter two felt that their supporters were not adequately represented in the Council. AJSU and JPP also did not join due to inadequate representation. The share of cake determined their attitude towards the new-born baby. Fractions, fragile and selfish nature of the leadership was openly exposed at intervals.

The Interim Council was to last only for six months and the new Council with 162 elected and 18 nominated members was to replace it within that period. Unfortunately, the elections are yet to be held. The six months period is already over.

According to the JAAC Act, 1994, the post of the Chairman shall be held by a tribal. All the MPs, MLAs and the MLCs from the Jharkhand region shall be the nominated members of the Council. It may be mentioned that a defeated member of the Parliament or Legislature automatically ceases to be the member of the Council. But some such ex-members attended the meeting of the Council and got the resolution passed as per their likings.[6]

The Jharkhand Area Autonomous Council have been given the charge of 40 subjects including agriculture, rural development, public works, public health, and minerals. The Council has the power to recommend for legislation to the Assembly through the State Government and to frame bylaws and regulations under the existing Acts. It has supervisory power over the Municipalities, Panchayat Samitis and Gram Panchayats within the area.[7]

It will have its own funds, including atleast 25 per cent of the State's plan fund's share.[8] The assets and staff of the three autonomous boards, which existed earlier, namely, the Santal Pargana Swashashi Parishad, Uttar Chotanagpur Swashashi Parishad and Dakshin Chotanagpur Swashashi Parishad has been put under the charge of JAAC.

It is true that JAAC could not have a happy beginning. The State Government displayed utter shortsightedness in the Constitution of the Interim Council and played politics. The weaknesses of the Jharkhand leaders were exposed. It is sad that manipulative politics continued to be played at the cost of the people of the country and Bihar. It is high time that the Government of Bihar does the following without further delay to save the situation from deterioration:

(i) initiate action to hold election to the Council; delimitate the constituencies as per Section 4 and 8 of the JAAC Act; complete the election process,
(ii) constitute permanent body,

(iii) transfer the departments to JAAC as per the Act,

(iv) restore administrative and financial powers to the Council as per the provision of the Act. It is a sad commentary on the whole affair that the Council does not have enough fund to open even the bank account.[9]

The Government of Bihar should do everything to see that JAAC does not remain a mere show piece. The JAAC remains a non-starter due to the shortsightedness of the Bihar Government. Sibu Soren revived the statehood demand only in six months time. He has even asked the people of the region to take up arms to achieve their objective.[10] Is he alone to be blamed?

The representatives of JMM (S), AJSU-JPP combine, JMM (Mardi), Jharkhand Party and CPI (ML) have agreed to form a United Jharkhand Front.[11] It is also reported that the emergence of a militant party, in collusion with the Naxalites, known as 'JMM (Nirmal) is on cards.[12] The Naxalites have been looking for the safe refuge in the inaccessible terrain of Saranda forest after massive crackdown in the Palamu and Chatra districts[13] and therefore, their tie up with the middle ranking leaders is possible. These developments may complicate the problem in near future.

REFERENCES

1. *The Hindustan Times*, Monday Extra, August 14, 1996, Amar Kumar Singh, Tough Tasks, Horny Tests.
2. *Frontline*, September 8, 1995, p. 40.
3. *Ibid.*
4. *The Telegraph*, June 28, 1995, p. 13. Tapas Chakraborty, *Demos Unscrupulous*.
5. *The Hindustan Times*, Monday Extra, August 7, 1996, *Will JAAC Spell Change*?
6. *The Hindustan Times*, August 18, 1996, p. 6.
7. *Frontline*, September 8, 1995, p. 40.
8. *Ibid.*
9. *India Today*, October 15, 1996, p. 86.
10. *The Hindustan Times*, July 2, 1996, p. 7, Editorial, *Setback to Jharkhand*.
11. *The Hindustan Times*, August 1, 1996, p. 1.
12. *Ibid.*
13. *The Telegraph*, June 28, 1995, p. 13, Tapas Chakraborty, *Demos Unscrupulous*.

13

AUTONOMOUS HILL COUNCIL IN LADAKH

IT was for the first time in the history of Jammu and Kashmir on June 6, 1995, that the angry Ladakhi leaders delivered speeches and shouted slogans against India and threatened to boycott the elections. The anti-India sentiment ran very high in Ladakh. The pacifist and peace-loving Ladakhis were angry, angry against India and not against the Kashmir Government. The unimaginative and short-sighted handling of their affairs in most casual way forced the Ladakhis to come to the streets of Leh with full-throated angry slogans. True to their tradition, the Central Government listened when the Ladakhis assumed agitational postures. The Ladakhis were assured of the formation of 'Autonomous Hill Council' more than once, but the real action was always stalled and the assurances forgotten. The slogan shouting and angry anti-India speeches catalysed action. Steps were taken to ensure the formation of Leh District Autonomous Hill Council.

The Ladakhis and the valley centred leadership of Kashmir never worked on the same wavelength. The two regions lacked adequate cultural, historical and emotional links. The only link between the Valley and the Ladakh, as the Ladakhis thought, was the Maharaja and the first thing Sheikh Abdullah did was to abolish kingship after 1952 accord with Pt. Nehru. The tie was snapped according to the Ladakhis.

Ladakh covered almost two-third geographical area of the State of Jammu & Kashmir, but sent only two MLAs in the State Legislative Assembly. Thus, while contributing maximum to the size of the State, Ladakh played only a limited marginal political role. The attitude of the people towards the Centre differed. Unlike the Valley, the separatist voice was never heard in Ladakh. The Ladakhis always wanted strong tie with the Centre.

The Ladakhis gradually developed bitterness towards the Centre and the State. Some of the reasons of the same are given below :

A Sketch Map

MAP 13.1 : Ladakh Region, Jammu & Kashmir

(i) It is alleged that there was systematic discrimination against the Ladakhis in the matters of development. Maximum allocation of Central funds were claimed and received for the development of Ladakh and utilized in the Valley.[1]

(ii) The Kashmiri leaders, starting from Sheikh Abdullah onwards, never seriously considered a scheme of inter-regional relations.[2]

(iii) The autonomy movements were not properly handled. The Kashmiri leaders applied force and allurement to the ambitious Ladakhi politicians to handle the situation.[3] Needless to say that they did not succeed in their game and the movement continued.

(iv) The Kashmiri leaders communalised the society and the politics of Ladakh to weaken it. Ladakh was partitioned into Leh and Kargil districts. The society was divided into Buddhist and Muslim. The Ladakhis were highly resentful. Sheikh initiated measures to create 'Greater Kashmir' by creating the districts of Kargil in Ladakh and Doda in Jammu.

(v) The Central Government persistently denied the benefit of rational reorganization of State to the Ladakhis; continued to ignore their demand for self-rule; pursued the policy of status-quoism and allowed the unitary status of the State to continue. The inter-regional tension was ignored by the Government of India.

(vi) The Ladakhi protests, criticism and the agitations continued to be directed against the Kashmir Government all these years. The communalisation of the politics resulted into the year long agitation and the boycott of the Muslims during 1989-90. The Ladakh Buddhist Association (LBA) spearheaded the violent agitation; gave a call to "free Ladakh from Kashmir" and demanded Union Territory status for Ladakh.[4] One year long agitation was followed by the discussions and mutual consultations between various parties. Finally, a tripartite agreement was arrived at between the representatives of the Ladakh Buddhist Association and that of the State and the Central Governments. Ladakh was promised an 'Autonomous Hill Council for Leh'. The demand for the Union Territory status was withdrawn by the Ladakh Buddhist Association. The social boycott observed against the Muslims since 1993 was also withdrawn by LBA. It may be mentioned that such boycott was observed by both the communities against each other.

The formation of a new Coordination Committee for Leh Autonomous Council (CCLC) followed the agreement. The persistent efforts of the CCLC brought result. The Government finally conceded the demand for the autonomous council for Leh, and also for Kargil if latter desires for the same. The demand was conceded on October 9, 1993. The Government, as usual, delayed the follow up action. This angered the people enormously and hence the incidence of March 6, 1995 mentioned above. This culminated into the announcement of poll boycott by the Ladakhis. The foreign media observed on the development thus:

"Indian exploitation, Indian inability to defend Ladakh and the weakness of the historical association between India and Ladakh carries the message that Ladakh like Kashmir should separate from India and go its own way."[5] India pays through the nose for the development of Jammu & Kashmir and yet was termed exploiter. The mishandling of Ladakh affair angered the Ladakhis. It is unfortunate that Indians have ceased to be angry over the short-sighted policy and apathy of the Central and the State Governments.

It took almost six years after the agitation was started in 1989, that the bill for the formation of the 'Autonomous Hill Council' was passed in the middle of 1995. The election for the Council was held soon after.

The Autonomous Hill Council for Leh is formed on the model and pattern of Darjeeling Autonomous Gorkha Hill Council. However, it will have more power than the latter with jurisdiction over the employment, development and other related activities. It would have the power to recruit non-gazetted employees in all the subjects, except the police and judiciary.[6]

There is provision for 26 elected and four nominated members in the Council. The nomination should be made from amongst the principal minorities and the women.[7] There was provision of the annual grant of Rs. 25 crores for the Council during the last financial year.

The leaders of the Kashmir Valley are never tired of asking for more autonomy. On the other hand they always silence the autonomy demands of Ladakh and Jammu. The Central Government always does, whatever the leadership of Kashmir Valley want. It is good that the problem of autonomy in Ladakh has been solved. The success of the experiment lies in the sincerity of all the three parties.

REFERENCES

1. Mishandling Ladakh May Prove Costly, P. Stobdan, *The Times of India*, Patna, April 5, 1995.
2. *Ibid.*
3. *Ibid.*
4. *Ibid.*
5. *Ibid.*
6. *The Hindustan Times*, Patna, July 3, 1995, p. 5.
7. *Ibid.*

LOW-KEY STATE DEMANDS

14

LOW-KEY STATE DEMANDS

THE country is facing the problem of unending 'State Demands' since independence. The States' Reorganization of 1956 could not satisfy many. The process of reorganization continued, unabated. The country has 25 States today. But it continues to have the demands for more States. The pending State demands may be categorised as given below:

(i) The demand which is going to be fulfilled very soon, such as, the Uttarakhand State demand.

(ii) The demands which persist inspite of the limited autonomy given, such as, the State demands in Jharkhand, Gorkhaland and Bodoland.

(iii) Theoretical demands in the mind of some intellectuals and a few politicians. The demands for such States have either been raised in very feeble voice or written in some magazines, newspapers or books. Such States include, Magadh, Bhojpuri Pradesh, Oudh, Maha-Koshal, Braj Pradesh, Mewar, Malwa, Kuchchh, Saurashtra, Rohilkhand, Udayachal, Kamtapur, etc. The demand for Seemanchal voiced by a politician may also come in this category.

(iv) Low key State demands in Chhattisgarh, Bundelkhand, Vidarbha, Telengana, etc. I shall deal with the demands of this category in this chapter. The demand for the States is not new in these areas. Often, some persons, mostly politicians, voice the demand for statehood, even organise rallies, raise slogans, get tired and stop. The lack of active public support often demoralises them.

The Prime Minister's recent announcement regarding the formation of Uttarakhand has encouraged many to restart the movements in their respective regions for new States. The 'Sangharsh Samitis' have already

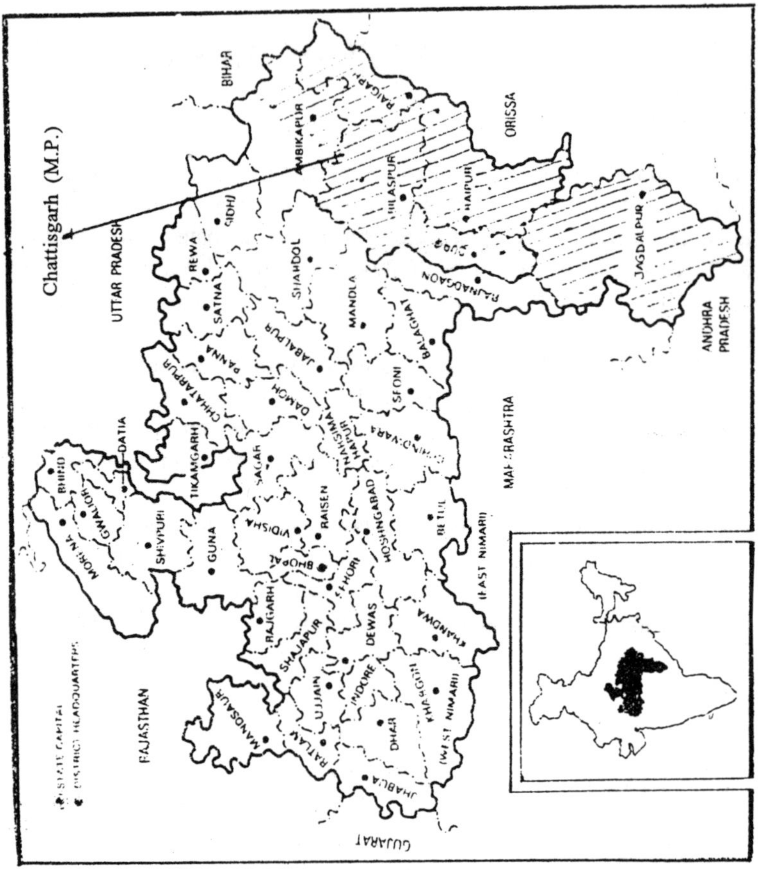

MAP 14.1 : Chhattisgarh, Madhya Pradesh

A Sketch Map

been formed in many regions for the purpose. Such developments in some of the States are discussed below:

Chhattisgarh

The districts of Raipur, Surguja, Durg, Rajnandgaon, Raigarh, Bilaspur and Bastar of Madhya Pradesh have the total area of 1,28,724 sq. km. and total population of 1,57,26,888. The area is rich in agriculture, forests and minerals. The area is known as the 'rice bowl of Central India'. It has 65 per cent of the forest cover, 30 per cent of the land area, and provides 35 to 40 per cent of the State income of Madhya Pradesh. The nature is generous with the region; man is not. About five lakhs people of the region migrate for five months every year to places like Punjab and Haryana for jobs. Chhattisgarh follows Bihar.

The demand for the separate State was made in Chhattisgarh during 1950s. The issue got prominence in 1977 also when the youth of the region were inspired by Pawan Diwan, a prominent and very popular person of the region to fight for the cause. Both the Congress (I) and the BJP promised statehood to the region in their 1993 election manifestoes. Madhya Pradesh Assembly unanimously passed a resolution last year to approach the Centre for the creation of the Chhattisgarh State. The demand is still pending with the Centre. In the meantime, the creation of Uttarakhand was announced and the leaders of Chhattisgarh movement have announced to form 'Azad Chhattisgarh Fouz' for the statehood struggle. The movement have every chance to hot up in near future.

There are some inherent weaknesses in the movement also which are given below:

(i) The Chhattisgarh State demand is mainly confined to the urban areas of Durg, Raipur and Bilaspur. The movement is yet to spread and grow roots in the smaller towns and rural areas.
(ii) Certain groups would like Raigarh and Surguja to join Jharkhand, rather than Chhattisgarh.
(iii) Naxalites want Dandakaranya State in and around Bastar.
(iv) There is considerable sub-regional disparity within the Chhattisgarh region in matters of growth of industries and irrigation facilities. This is an apparent inner weakness of the region.
(v) The cracks within the movement may cause failure of the movement.[1] The cracks have taken place in other autonomy movements also, such as in Bodoland Movement. The options

A Sketch Map

MAP 14.2 : Bundelkhand Region, Uttar Pradesh

of smaller districts and tribal autonomy[2] may also have some takers. Such options are already under consideration, if we take the area, population and the natural resources of the region into consideration, then the economic viability of the State cannot be questioned. However, other rational parameters of the statehood also need thorough scrutiny.

Bundelkhand

Bundelkhand region has the districts of Chatarpur, Tikamgarh, Shivpuri, Gwalior, Datia and Bhind of Madhya Pradesh and the district of Banda, Hamirpur, Jalaun, Jhansi and Lalitpur of Uttar Pradesh. The total area of these districts is 65,141 sq. kms. (35,724 sq. kms. in Madhya Pradesh and 29,417 sq. kms. in Uttar Pradesh). The total population is 1, 29,67,720 (62,58,566 in Madhya Pradesh and 67,09,154 in Uttar Pradesh).

Bundelkhand is a development starved region of Madhya Pradesh and Uttar Pradesh. The demand for the statehood was casually raised. The public support was lacking in the past, although protest meetings and *dharnas* were frequently organized in the past.

The Prime Minister's announcement about Uttarakhand and the recently held elections catalysed action. The leaders of different parties and all hues and shades took active part in recently organized Jhansi demonstration for carving out separate Bundelkhand State.[3]

Unlike Uttaranchal, Vananchal and Chhattisgarh demands, the Bharatiya Janata Party have not pronounced its stand on Bundelkhand. However, Ms. Uma Bharati and Ganga Charan Rajput, BJP MP, took active part in the recently held demonstrations.[4] Narayan Dutt Tiwari have openly supported the statehood demand. He was a candidate in the recent election from Jhansi and was fifth in the race.[5]

Telangana

The Telangana region of Andhra Pradesh was a part of Nizam's Hyderabad State. The nine Telangana districts were merged with Andhra Pradesh on November 1, 1956. Hyderabad, the capital of Andhra Pradesh falls under Telangana region. The total area of the districts of Adilabad, Hyderabad, Ranga Reddy, Karimnagar, Khaman, Mahaboob Nagar, Medak, Nalgonda, Nizamabad and Warrangal is 1,14,863 sq. kms. The total population according to 1991 census is 2,59,75,506.

The area suffers from poverty, inequality and the lack of proper development. A violent Communist movement was started in the area

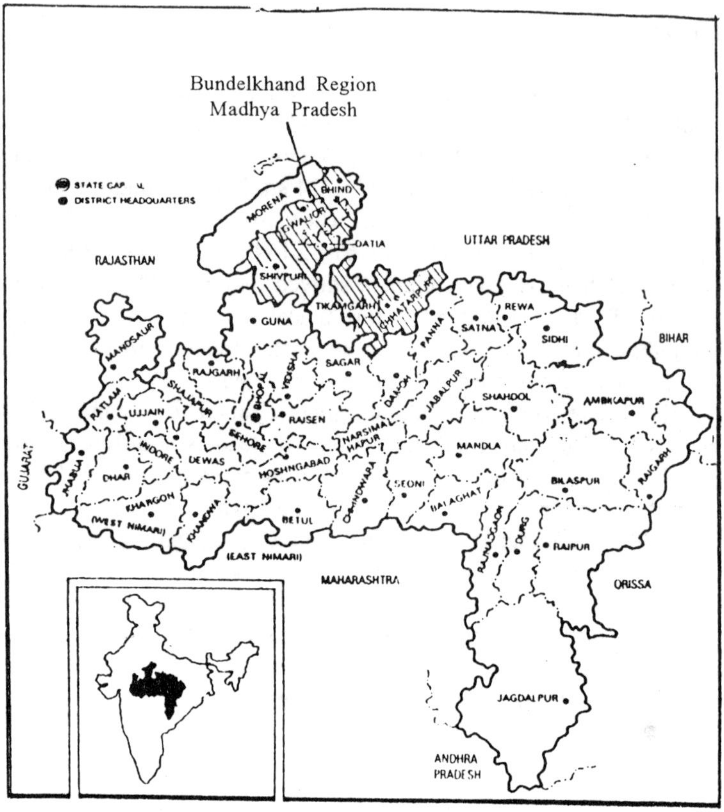

A Sketch Map

MAP 14.3 : Bundelkhand Region, Madhya Pradesh

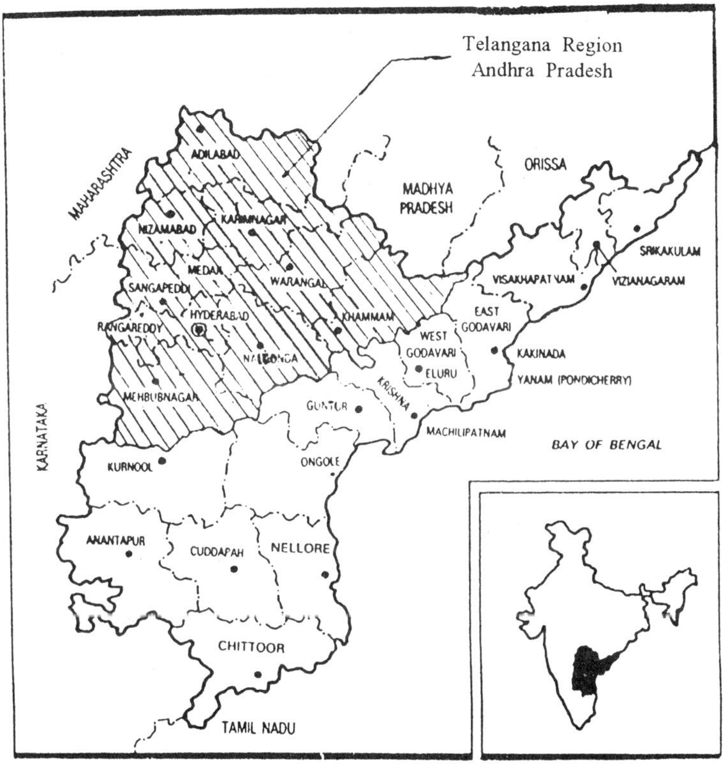

A Sketch Map

MAP 14.4 : Telangana Region, Andhra Pradesh

just after independence. The various People's War Group Naxalite groups continue to have their hold in Telangana region.

The demand for the separation of Telangana from Andhra Pradesh was started in 1969 by Dr. M. Chenna Reddy. Mrs. Gandhi solved the problem during her premiership. The demand has resurfaced recently. Nayani Narasimha Reddy, President, Janata Dal, Andhra Pradesh was the first person to voice the demand and to send a memorandum recently to the Prime Minister for the creation of Telangana. The memorandum was sent through S. Jaipal Reddy, MP (Rajya Sabha). He has his own interpretation of the PM's announcement on Uttarakhand. According to him, it implied in principle the acceptance of the concept of smaller States which are administratively more viable.[6]

A group has also emerged within the ruling Telugu Desam Party under the leadership of Bharat Simha Reddy, MLA. The group has informal approach. They do not want to be left behind and face the people's anger. Most of the MLAs of Congress (I) and partymen from Telengana region are for the Telangana cause, although the Party has not taken any official stand on the issue. Both TDP and Congress (I) supporters of Telengana cause want either statehood or autonomy within the Andhra Pradesh.

The students of various colleges of Kakatiya University brought out processions for Telengana State and the political leaders have not ignored the signal. They would like to derive benefit from the upsurge of popular emotion of the youth of Telengana.[7]

Telengana remained undeveloped. The successive State Governments blamed the Naxalite outfits for the backwardness of the region. Is it not true that the Naxals could succeed because the Government failed to bring development?

Vidarbha

Vidarbha is the Eastern part of Maharashtra. It has the districts of Buldana, Akola, Amarawati, Yavatmal, Wardha, Nagpur, Bhandara, Chandrapur and Gadchiroli with total geographical area of 97,409 sq. kms. The population of the region is 1,73,91,134. The region is comparatively less developed than Western Maharashtra.

The Vidarbha was a part of the former Madhya Pradesh which had its capital at Nagpur in the Vidarbha region. The seventeen Hindi speaking districts remained with Madhya Pradesh and merged with Madhya Bharat, Vindhya Pradesh and Bhopal to give Madhya Pradesh a new shape, as per the recommendations of SRC and the States

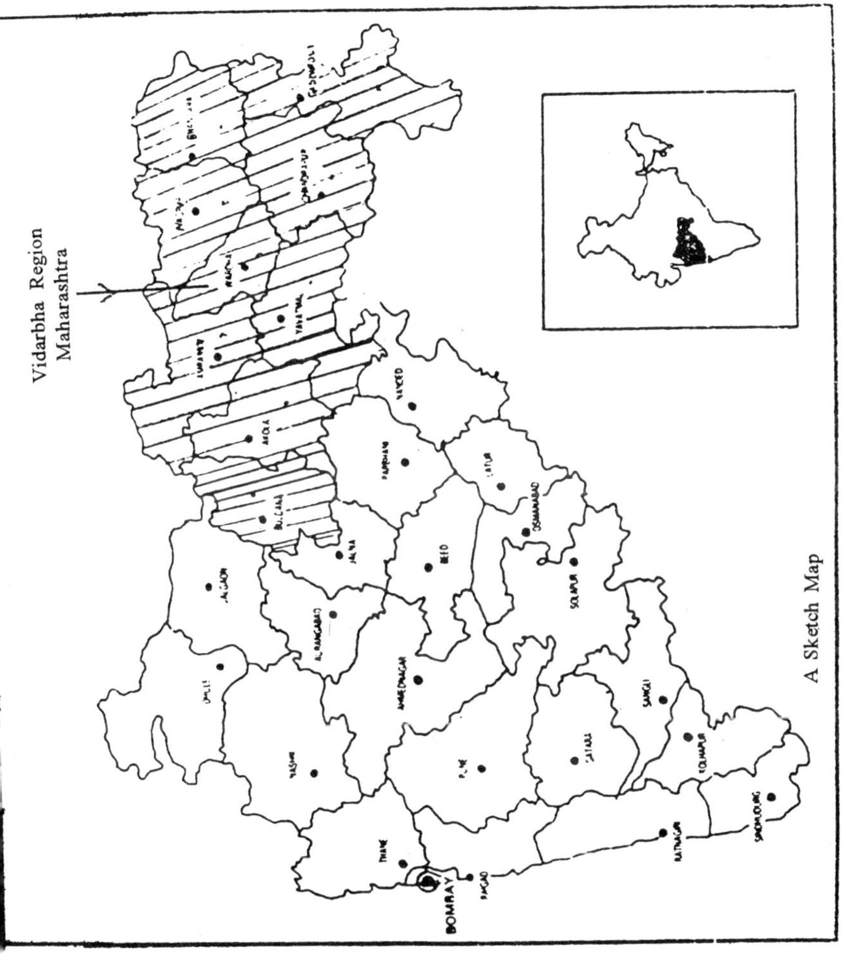

MAP 14.5 : Vidarbha Region, Maharashtra

Reorganization Act, 1956. Nine Marathi speaking districts of Vidarbha were merged with the Marathi speaking Bombay province. Of course, Bombay remained a bilingual State upto April 1960. The SRC recommended the formation of Vidarbha State in 1956, but the same was not formed.

The demand for Vidarbha State is not new. The separation is sought on the name of under development of the region.

PM's announcement on Uttarakhand has enthused the protagonists of Vidarbha State also. Vidarbha Rajya Sunghursh Samiti is mobilising the support of the local politicians for the statehood. Samawaya Samiti is the common platform of the politicians working for the purpose of attainment of statehood.[8]

Among the political parties, the Janata Dal, the Bharatiya Janata Party and the various factions of the Republican party are in favour of the statehood. The Shiv Sena opposes the idea.[9] The party leadership has opposed the formation of Vidarbha in no uncertain terms. The Congress also does not believe in the separation of Vidarbha from Maharashtra.[10] Shankar Rao Chawan is opposed to the idea of bifurcation of Maharashtra.[11] However, there is change in the attitude of the Congress (I) on this issue. A delegation, led by former Union Minister Basant Sathe, met the Prime Minister and the Congress President, Sitaram Kesri and submitted a memorandum to the P.M. and the copy of the memorandum to Mr. Kesri. The members of the delegation were N.K.P. Salve, Datta Meghe, Vilas Muttewar, and Mukul Wasnik. The memorandum was signed by CWC members K. Karunakaran, Balram Jakhar, Ghulam Nabi Azad, Rajesh Pilot, and General Secretaries of the Party, Sudhakarrao Naik and Ahmed Patel. The delegation urged the Prime Minister for creation of Vidarbha State.[12] Thus there is change in the stand of Congress (I) about the Vidarbha issue. The leaders feel that the movement for the creation of State will revive the fortunes of the Congress (I). It may bring a political crisis for the ruling combine of Maharashtra.[13] It may be pointed out that a resolution for the creation of the new State was passed in a Congress Workers Conference held in Nagpur on September 15, 1996. The Congress leaders have proposed to start a peaceful and non-confrontationist agitation for statehood. It may be started from 'Sindh Khed Raja' the birth place of Shivaji's mother.[14]

As stated above, Shiv Sena is opposed to the creation of Vidarbha but the local MP Umesh Jhadgaonkar has expressed his sympathy for the cause.[15]

The Prime Minister has expressed his willingness to consider the demand for separate State if the Congressmen get clearance from the

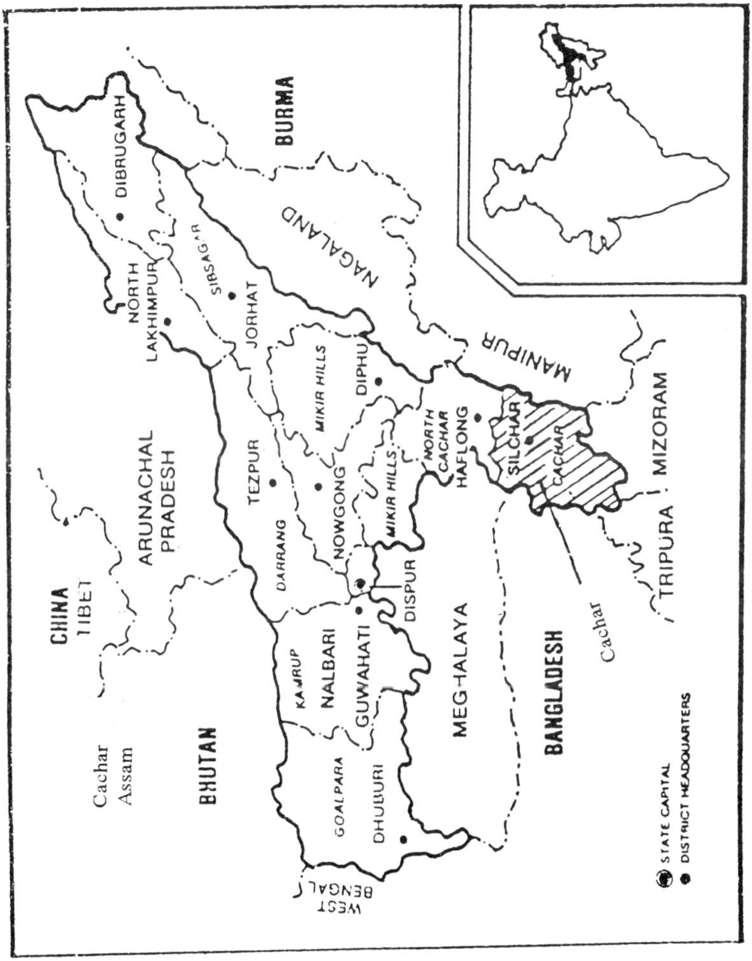

A Sketch Map MAP 14.6 : Cachar, Assam

Congress President, Sitaram Kesri. He reminded the Congress delegates that the demand of Uttarakhand was met due to the letter written by Mr. Narasimha Rao, the then Congress President to him. Mr. Rao wrote for Union Territory status, but the PM offered statehood to the Uttarakhandis.[16]

Malwa

The demand for Malwa is also heard in Madhya Pradesh now a days.

Seemanchal

The demand for the State has been made recently. The topic is fully discussed elsewhere in this book.

Cachar

The three Barak Valley districts of Cachar, Karimnagar and Hailakandi have total area of 8,267.3 sq. kms. and the total population of 24,90,009 according to the 1991 Census. The region is predominantly Bengali speaking. The region has a Central University, A Regional Engineering College and a Regional Medical College. All the institutions are located in Silchar. The State of Assam is bilingual and the demand for Union Territory status for Cachar is occasionally heard.

REFERENCES

1. Re-mapping the Country, *India Today*, October 15, 1996, p. 87.
2. *Ibid.*
3. *The Hindustan Times*, Patna, September 22, 1996, p. 5.
4. *Ibid.*
5. *Ibid.*
6. Bobby John Varkey, States on a platter? *The Hindustan Times*, Patna, Sunday Magazine; September 8, 1996.
7. *Ibid.*
8. *Ibid.*
9. *Ibid.*
10. *Ibid.*
11. *The Hindustan Times*, September 30, 1996.
12. *Ibid.*
13. *Ibid.*
14. *Ibid.*
15. Bobby John Varkey, *op. cit.*
16. *The Hindustan Times*, September 30, 1996.

15

AUTONOMY DEMANDS IN JAMMU AND LADAKH

THE State of Jammu and Kashmir consists of three distinct regions. These regions differ widely in many respects. The Jammu region was given to Maharaja Gulab Singh by Maharaja Ranjit Singh in 1846. He received Kashmir as a result of Amritsar Treaty in 1846 after the war of Sobranw. The Ladakh region was won and incorporated in his kingdom afterwards.

The Kashmir Valley has an area of 15,948 sq. kms. and the population of 31,34,904 according to 1991 census. It has six districts, namely Srinagar, Anantnag, Badgam, Baramula, Kupwara and Pulwama. About 3.5 lakh Hindus were forced to leave the valley due to terrorism in 1989-90. Majority of the people of the valley are Muslims. The language of the valley is Kashmiri, but Urdu is the State language.

The six districts of Jammu, namely, Jammu, Udhampur, Doda, Kathua, Poonch, and Rajauri have the total area of 26,293 sq. kms. and the population of 27,18,113. The language spoken by the people is Dogri. Jammu is a Hindu majority region of the State.

The third region of the State of Jammu and Kashmir is Ladakh. It has two districts namely, Leh and Kargil with the total area of 96,701 sq. kms. and the population of 1,24,372. The Leh district with predominantly Buddhist population is the biggest district of the country with an area of 82,665 sq. kms. Thc language is Ladakhi.

The instrument of accession of the State with India was signed on October 27,1947. The State was irrevocable brought under the permanent territorial and constitutional jurisdiction of India as per Article I of the Constitution of India adopted on January 26, 1950. A special provision was made for the State under Article 370, in Part XXI; Temporary and Transitional Provisions. The Union Parliament has the power to make law on any topic under the Union and Concurrent lists. In case of the State of Jammu and Kashmir, the concurrence of the State Government

A Sketch Map

MAP 15.1 : Jammu Region, Jammu & Kashmir

is necessary for making law on such subjects, except in the case of Defence, Foreign Affairs and Communications.

Dr. Ambedkar opposed the insertion of the Article.[1] However, it was inserted due to the assertion of Nehru. Nehru, himself, called it a temporary and unusual provision in the Parliament in July 24, 1952.[2] Sheikh Abdullah had series of meetings with Nehru to evolve a working relation resulting into so called Delhi Agreement (July 1952). He got special citizenship rights for the Kashmiris, a dual citizenship right. A Kashmiri can fight election anywhere in the country and may acquire property anywhere. A non-Kashmiri is not allowed to do so in Kashmir. The State got separate flag and separate Constitution apart from the national flag and the Constitution of India. The Kashmiri women marrying non-Kashmiris, even get forfeited the properties in the valley and the right of admission in the Medical and Engineering colleges.[3] Such discriminations continued inspite of the most favoured treatment given to the State by the Central Government. Everything worked against the emotional, constitutional, legal, administrative, economic, social and cultural integration of the State with rest of the country. Jammu and Ladakh wanted greater integration with the country: a section of the population of Kashmir Valley wanted just the opposite. Unfortunately, Delhi saw from the eyes of this section and heard from the ears of the same. A classic example of obsession with religion and secular pretention of the ruling elite of this country. After all, the Kashmir Valley differed in no other way from the rest of the country, except for the fact that the valley had majority Muslim population. Unlike, Pakistan and Bangladesh, India did not discriminate against its religious minorities.

Perceptional Differences

Sheikh Abdullah organised the people of Kashmir Valley against the Maharaja during the pre-independence days under the banner of Muslim Conference. The Muslim Conference became National Conference later on. The organization working in the Jammu region was Jammu Praja Parishad, which merged with Bharatiya Jan Sangh later on. The perceptions of the political elite of the two regions, their *modus operandi*, organizations, everything differed. All the princely States of the country were merged together or with the neighbouring States or reorganized within a decade after independence. The same yardstick was not applied in the case of Jammu and Kashmir. The State was denied the benefits of reorganisation. The voice for autonomy became louder and louder in the State. It demanded more autonomy, but always suppressed the autonomy demands of the Jammu and the Ladakh regions.[4]

Discrimination against Jammu and Ladakh

The leaders of Jammu and Ladakh have many grievances against the Valley dominated leadership of the State and the Central Government. Some of their grievances and the acts of discrimination are highlighted below:

(i) They allege that they are subjected to discrimination in the matter of development. The proposals are sent to Delhi for development funds, in which the needs of other regions are duly projected. But, a lot of money sanctioned on the name of the development of other regions is spent in the Kashmir Valley. It may be mentioned that 75 per cent of the fund spent comes from Delhi, out of which 90 per cent is Central assistance and 10 per cent loan.[5] The State mobilises only 25 per cent revenue. The per capita Central assistance was Rs. 1122.00 during 1989-90 as against Rs. 109 for Bihar, 91 for U.P. and Rs. 67 for West Bengal for that period.[6] The State also receives cheapest subsidised rice in the country.

(ii) *Political Dominance of the Valley* over two other regions is strongly resented by the latter. The Ladakh has almost two-third of the geographical area of the State. The area of Jammu is far more than that of the valley and it has comparable, rather, only slightly less population than that in the valley. These factors are ignored and they get proportionately lesser representation in the Assembly and the Parliament. The Census operation was stopped in Jammu & Kashmir in 1991. The people of Jammu protested strongly against the act. This was done due to pressure exerted by the National Conference leaders and Mufti Mohammad Said, former Union Home Minister. The population of the valley decreased due to exodus of the Hindus from the Valley, and there was every likelihood that the number of Assembly seats for Jammu was to become more than that of the Valley. Similar act was seen during 1951 census also and the delimitation of Assembly seats was done according to the population figures of 1941 census. Not only this, Sheikh Abdullah rejected the nominations of the candidates of Jammu Praja Parishad in 1951 elections and stalled their entry in the State Assembly, which turned into Constituent Assembly of the State soon after. Thus he thwarted the voice of Jammu in deciding the future of the State.

Jammu was subjected to discrimination during 1961-71 also.

The population of Kashmir was 18 lakhs and that of Jammu was 16 lakhs according to 1961 census. Kashmir elected three MPs (one MP for every six lakh population) and Jammu elected only two (one for every eight lakh population). The situation did not change after 1971 census. The people of Jammu elected one MLA for every 67741 persons, while the Valley people elected one MLA for only 53288 persons. Such discriminatory actions continued and the people of Jammu and Ladakh suffered.

(iii) The people of other two regions also blame the State Government for communal divide in the State. The division of Udhampur into Doda and Udhampur, and Ladakh into Leh and Kargil was resented by the people. What is going on in Doda by the militants is deplorable and not difficult to understand. The whole game is aimed at disturbing the demographic texture of the district. The beginning was made by Sheikh Abdullah himself, who divided Udhampur. He also settled Muslim refugees in Jammu.

The Jammu & Kashmir has three regions, each with distinct culture, language, topography, etc. The forced unitary State on the people of Jammu and Ladakh is not going to benefit the country and the people of Jammu and Kashmir. Jammu wants separate identity. Ladakh wanted Union Territory status. The Leh Autonomous Hill Council has already started functioning.

The Gujjars are declared as Scheduled Tribe. They number ten lakhs and they deserve one Reserved Scheduled Tribe seat in the Parliament. The Punjabi speaking area of Uri Tithwal may pose a problem. It may join Jammu or Kashmir in the frame of divided State. Jammu is strategically located. The people of the region always wanted the closest tie with the Centre. The people of Jammu should not be made to feel that they are made to pay for their centripetal attitude. The State of Jammu and Kashmir should become full-fledged States and Ladakh should be made an Union Territory. It is high time to reorganize the State along rational parameters.

REFERENCES

1. *Aaj* (Hindi, Patna), Kashmir Special, April 18, 1993, p. 2.
2. Autonomy for Kashmir, Jagmohan on its Pitfalls, *The Hindustan Times*, August 15, 1996.
3. *Aaj*, op. cit.
4. *Ibid.*
5. *Ibid.*
6. *Ibid.*

16

THE DEMAND FOR THE MITHILA STATE

DR. Jagannath Mishra sharply reacted when the opinion to separate Jharkhand from Bihar was expressed by S.B. Chawan, the then Home Minister of India. He vehemently opposed the idea of separation of Jharkhand. The same person, Dr. Jagannath Mishra, former Chief Minister of Bihar has changed his stand in an unbelievable way and proposed for the creation of Jharkhand and Mithila States. Nothing has changed in Bihar and in Mithilanchal in the last 3-4 years, except for the Prime Minister, H.D. Deve Gowda's announcement about the creation of Uttarakhand and the prospect of the bleak political future of Dr. Mishra and that of the Congress (I) party. The political calculation, rather than the needs of the regions, seems to be the motivating factor.

Bihar has the rich combination of fertile North and Central Bihar and the mineral rich Southern plateau. It sent 54 MPs to the National Parliament. The same Jagannath Mishra was the Chief Minister for many many years and had the opportunity to develop Mithilanchal. He failed to do so inspite of the opportunity in his hand. If Dr. Mishra failed to develop a resource rich Bihar, then how he hopes to perform the feat with moth-eaten, resource starved, development and power starved, flood-ravaged North Bihar? Dr. Mishra knows it better.

This country has the rich crop of pressure groups and the elite fora. They talk, organise movements, gauze the mood of the persons in power and act. Given the opportunity, such organizations immediately spring to action, girdle the loin for movement keeping the possibility of success in mind. Unlawful organizations, private Senas and criminal elements also cease the opportunity and add the elements of violence. The incidence of burning and looting a whole train on the issue of Broad Guaze conversion of Darbhanga-Samastipur line is not even one year old. The Central and the State Governments always send a wrong signal that the pressure works and the violence pays. This is a factor on which the

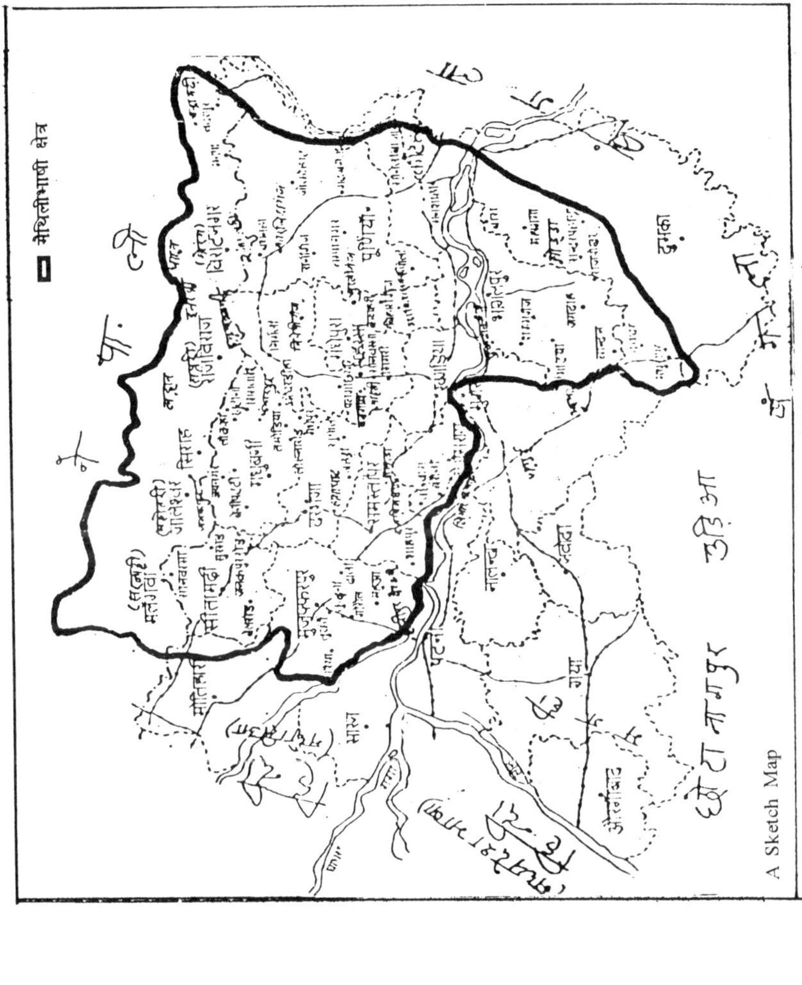

MAP 16.1 : Mithilanchal Demand

Source : Maithili speaking areas according to the Linguistic Survey of India.

agitationists, mostly rely. Movement for separate Mithila State may also follow this pattern.

The Mithilanchal Vikash Congress demanded the formation of an Autonomous Development Council for the Mithila region in July, 1996. Obviously, they were inspired by the formation of the Jharkhand Area Autonomous Council in Bihar. The demand for the formation of a separate Jharkhand State continued inspite of the formation of the JAAC. This encouraged the Mithila Rajya Sangharsh Samiti to initiate the mass contact campaign for Mithila State in March 1996.

The Maithil Mahasabha has announced its agitational programmes for the attainment of the goal of separate Mithila State. It may be pointed out that the demand for separate Mithila State was made in the late 1930s by the same Maithil Mahasabha with the support of the then Maharaja of Darbhanga. The movement died out due to the lack of popular support and resurfaced only after the independence.

Apart from the above-mentioned organizations, some other organizations have also started taking part in the nascent State demand movement. The Vidyapati Seva Sansthan (VSS) have announced the action programme. The Mithila Vikash Parishad have hailed the announcements of the Prime Minister on Uttarakhand and that of Dr. Mishra on the formation of a Mithila State.

The Janata Dal has a very strong presence in Mithilanchal. The Party and its leader and the Bihar Chief Minister, Shri Laloo Prasad Yadav strongly opposes any move to bulkanize Bihar. The other political parties have not taken any stand. But, the future is going to be murkier and hazier no doubt.

Dr. Laksman Jha took the initiative and started the movement for the formation of Mithila State just after independence. His demand covered the area of the Maithili Language shown in the Linguistic Survey of India of George Abraham Grierson. It roughly covered the Bihar, North of the Ganges minus the Bhojpuri speaking areas; the districts of Bhagalpur, Banka, Godda and Deoghar and the Sarlahi, Saptari, Mahotary, Morang, Bara, Rautahat and Parsa areas of Nepal. Some Congressmen, under the leadership of Jankinandan Singh also participated in the movement inspite of the opposition by the Congress Party and the Bihar Government.

The demand for a Mithila State was basically a linguistic State demand. The area of the Maithili language has been highly reduced in the last few decades due to the assertion of the Bajjika and the Angika identities. The inhabitants of the Muzaffarpur, Vaishali, Sitamarhi

Sheohar and part of Samastipur claim Bajjika as their mother tongue. Similarly, the inhabitants of Bhagalpur, Banka, Katihar, Madhepura, Purnia etc. talk of the Angika language. The protagonists of Mithila State often ignore this aspect of the change of perception.

The recent demand for the Seemanchal with the claim for the same area has further complicated the matter. The Seemanchal protagonist has not only claimed the Purnia and Koshi divisions, but even the Darbhanga division, which forms the core of Mithilanchal.

The Angika and the Bajjika dialects have greatly reduced the area of Maithili. This makes the demand for the Mithila State unrealistic and uneconomic. Nevertheless, the issue has the potential to be highly emotive and needs proper sensible handling. The demand for Mithila State has the potential of catalysing similar claims for Bhojpuri State, Angika State, Bajjika State and Magahi State in Bihar and tension and conflict for deciding their borders. The demand for Jharkhand continues to trouble the minds of the people. The demand persists inspite of the formation of Jharkhand Area Autonomous Council. Initially, the protagonists of small States may ask for Development Councils, but that may prove only to be the stepping stone for demanding statehood. We have examples to prove the statement. The experiments of giving autonomy within the framework of a State has failed in many States of this country.

Bihar has the classic combination of agriculture rich and mineral rich regions. The God and the Nature provided the State, what was denied to others. But the State could not develop. The State provides a classic example of failed opportunities. The Messiahs, who failed Bihar are reappearing with new prescriptions. Who will save the State from their evil designs?

17

THE STATEHOOD DEMAND IN KARBI-ANGLONG AND NORTH CACHAR HILLS

THE Assam has only two hill districts after the reorganization of the North-East India and the resultant dismemberment of the State. The area and the population of the two districts is given below:

District	*Area (in sq. km.)*	*Population (1991)*	*Headquarters*
Karbi Anglong	10,332	6,55,415	Diphu
North Cachar Hills	4,890	1,49,346	Haflong
Total	15,222	8,04,761	

These districts enjoyed autonomy under Sixth Schedule. Both the districts have their separate District Councils. The demand for the creation of the Eastern Hill State was made at Shillong in the meeting of the members of the Executive Committees of the District Councils on June 16, 1954. The Mikir Hills (now Karbi Anglong) District Council did not attend the meeting. The members of the North-Cachar Hills and the Lushai Hills District Councils opposed the creation of the Eastern Hill State and asked for more autonomy to the District Councils by amending the Sixth Schedule. These districts welcomed maximum district level autonomy offers of the Pataskar Commission and the Mehta Plan. The two districts were allowed the option to join the 'Autonomous State of Meghalaya' in 1970, but preferred to remain with Assam. The All Party Hill Leaders Conference, which spearheaded the movement for the separation of a Hill State from Assam, had no followers in the two districts and there was practically no movement for the separation of these two districts from Assam till Meghalaya was born and the District Council elections were held in 1971.

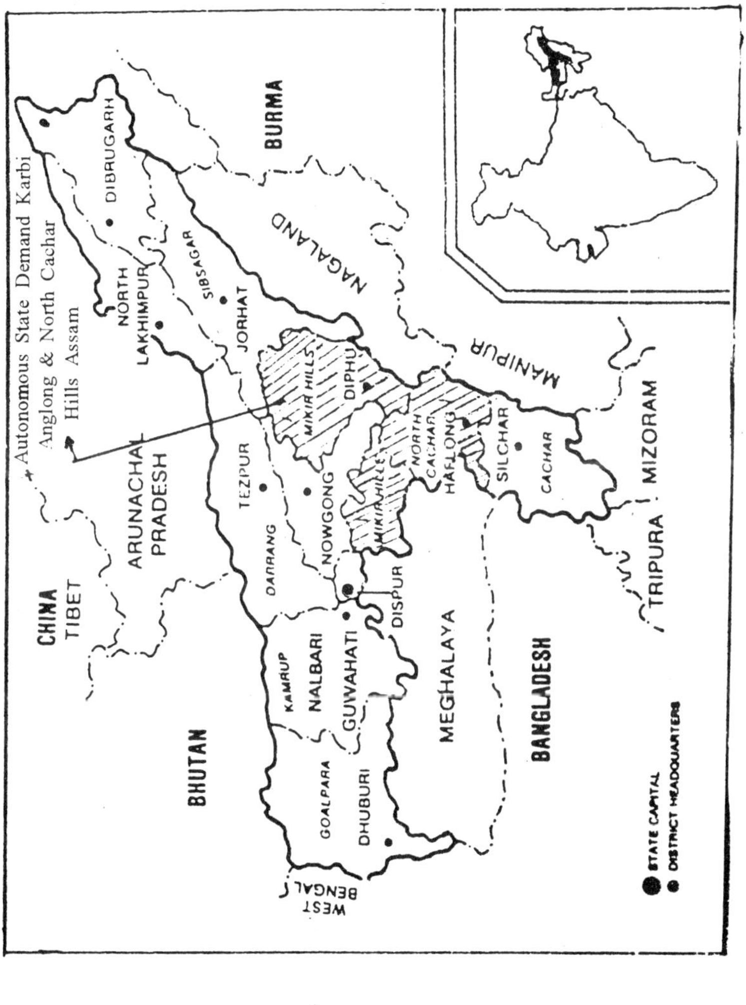

MAP 17.1 : Autonomous State Demand Karbi-Anglong & North Cachar Hills, Assam

The Congress Party had understanding with the Karbi-A-Darbar Party from the very beginning. The Congress used to fight Assembly and Parliament elections with the help of Karbi-A-Darbar and in turn used to help the latter in the District Council elections. This combination was beneficial for both the Parties for almost 26 years. The combination successfully foiled the attempt of the APHLC to incorporate Karbi Anglong district in the State of Meghalaya.

The leaders of the Mikir Hills unit of APHLC formed a new party, called 'Mikir Hills Progressive Party' in 1971. The Party had no economic programme and wanted English as the official language. The party, as is obvious, lacked organizational base. It wanted to break the monopoly of Congress-Karbi-A-Darbar combine in the district politics, as well as the monopoly of a few families in the same.[1] They fielded candidates for District Council elections in all the constituencies, but could win only two seats, due to the popularity of the candidates concerned and not due to the party's work or popularity. One of the winning candidates defected later on to join the Executive Committee of the District Council. The demoralised party leaders formed Mikir Hills 'Nationalist Organization' in 1972. The Party aimed at the merger of Mikir Hills with Nagaland. It failed to achieve its objective inspite of the help received from the Nagaland.

The United Karbi Nationalist Organization was established in 1973. The Party demanded the creation of a separate State. However, it very soon ceased to exist.

The All Party People's Conference was formed by the frustrated Congress (I) leaders of the district in 1978. Many of the Congress (I) leaders lost the elections due to the Janata Party wave. Some of them won, but did not get the share in power due to the obvious reason. Such leaders teamed up together, formed the party and demanded a separate full-fledged State by taking out Karbi Anglong and North Cachar Hills districts from Assam. The move was mainly due to the frustration of the leaders and the anger against the ruling Janata Party and therefore, lacked consistency.

Two frustrated politicians (one was removed from the post of the Chief Executive Member of the Karbi Anglong District Council and other was defeated in the Council election) formed a committee and demanded a separate State in 1980. The move did not succeed. A Separate State Demand Committee was formed in 1981. The leaders fought 1983 boycotted elections, got elected, were politically accommodated and forgot about the statehood. Dhoni Ram Rongpi was earlier the Chief Executive Member of the Karbi Anglong District Council and a Congress Party MLA in the Assam Assembly. He was the President of the above-mentioned Separate State Demand Committee.

The Assam Gana Parishad came to power in 1986. Dissatisfied Congress (I) leaders formed the Central Autonomous State Demand Committee at Haflong on May 5, 1986. A memorandum was submitted by the party to the Prime Minister on May 9, 1986 for the formation of the new State. After that, the party ceased to exist. Sonaram Thaosen the President and T. Nampui, the secretary of the organization belonged to North Cachar Hills. Biren Singh Engty, MP, Mangal Singh Engty, the Chief Executive Member, Karbi Anglong District Council and Rajen Timung, MLA were the Executive Members of the organization and they belonged to the Karbi Anglong district. Thus the Congress leaders of both the districts were involved in the formation of Central Autonomous State Demand Committee.

Two more organizations were born in the same year. The Autonomous State Demand Committee (ASDC) was formed on May 17, 1986. The Karbi Anglong North Cachar Hills Autonomous State Demand Committee (KANCHADCOM) was formed on May 25, 1986. These two parties have parallel organizations. The first one was opposed to the inclusion of the Congress-Karbi-A-Darbar alliance's participation in the ASDC. The KANCHADCOM wanted the broad alliance of the parties and the inclusion of the Congress in its organizational frame. Both the parties have sound organizations, the branches and the sub-branches spread over the entire area.

A broad based Central Committee supervises and controls the activities of the ASDC. It has branches, then sub-branches and finally the village branches. A village branch has control over 5-6 villages. The Volunteer Units function under the control of the village branch. The KANCHADCOM has a Central Committee, Sub-divisional Committees with five regions each and ten branches in each of the regions. They have a branch practically in every village. Like Congress-Karbi-A-Darbar alliance, the two parties mentioned above have strong organizational base.

The ASDC participated in the District Council elections in 1989 and won 22 seats out of total 26. The KANCHADCOM did not participate in the Council elections.

The ASDC and the KANCHADCOM added vigour and momentum to the autonomous State demand agitation. The frequent *bandhs* including the '*Rail Roko*' agitations and '*Road-blockades*' caused immense suffering to the people of Nagaland and Manipur. The supply-line of these States was frequently disrupted. The N.F. Railway was quick enough to cancel trains. The disruption in public life is too frequent and very annoying for the common man. The Governments of the North-

Eastern States have learnt to live with the absurdities caused by the parties and the pressure groups. The agitations, *bundhs*, conflicts and violence have become the way of life for them.

The Parties mentioned above lacked ideology; have no economic, social and cultural policies and have the single point programme of agitation for the autonomous State. Most of the parties wanted English as the official language. This was a part of the process of social distancing from the Assamese.

The political opportunism was very apparent in the behaviour of a large number of political activists attached to these parties. The involvement of a large number of the leaders in autonomy movements was not due to their commitment to the cause of the society or the tribe(s). It was really due to their personal frustration.

The centre of intense agitational activities of the ASDC and the KANCHADCOM is the Karbi Anglong. The North Cachar plays the supporting role. There is very high percentage of non-tribal, non-Karbi and non-Dimasa population in these districts. Both ASDC and KANCHADCOM are Karbi and Dimasa centred parties. The Mikir Hills Minority Party was the party of the non-Karbis in Karbi Anglong district. It was born when the APHLC activists started forcible land grabbing drive in an area inhabited mostly by the non-tribals. The Party ceased to be active after the Karbi Anglong decided not to join Meghalaya. The separatist parties should assure non-tribals and the tribals other than the Karbis and the Dimasas of their safe stay and justice. This, however, does not mean that the demand for a separate State does not defy the logic which should be the basis of any State demand.

REFERENCE

1. The Karbi Anglong district and North Cachar Hills district sent one MP to the Lok Sabha. There are four Assembly seats in the Karbi Anglong district. The Karbi Anglong District Council has the posts of the Chief Executive Member (CEM), Chairman, Executive Members (EM) and the Members. There was a group of personalities in the Karbi Anglong district related by blood.

   Khor Singh Terang was the MLA and the Chief Executive Member of the District Council. Chatra Singh Teron, ex-Minister, ex-CEM and ex-Chairman; Chandra Singh Teron, ex-CEM and ex-Chairman and Mohon Singh Teron were his son-in-laws. Soi Soi Terang, ex-Deputy-Minister and ex-Chairman was his younger brother. Sarthe Singh Terang ex-EM was his son. Dhoni Ram Rongpi, ex-CEM and ex-Minister is the brother-in-law of Chandra Singh Teron and Mohan Singh Teron. Sam Singh Hanse ex-Health Minister of Assam was his nephew. Joy Singh Doloi ex-CEM is the father-in-law of his younger brother.

THE NEW DEMAND

18

AND NOW SEEMANCHAL

MR. Taslimuddin, former Minister of State for Home has made a demand for a 'Seemanchal State' just a fortnight after his unceremonious forced exit from the Union Council of Ministers. He has vowed to launch agitation for the same with effect from September 1996. When reminded about the strong negative stand of the Chief Minister, Shri Laloo Prasad Yadav, Mr. Taslimuddin said, *"Laloo hamare Paigambar nahin hain. Ham chahenge ki is kshetra ka vikash karayen. Jab tak prant nahin, vikash nahin hoga."* (Laloo is not my messiah. It would like to get this area developed by him. Unless and until separate State is created, the area would not develop.)[1] Taslimuddin asserted that the Chief Minister would concede the demand 'under pressure.'[2]

The area claimed for the new State include the northern and north-eastern districts of Bihar on Indo-Nepal and West Bengal borders. The flood-ravaged development starved districts of North Bihar have suffered in many ways in last five decades. The communication network has not developed. Industrialization has not taken place. The power position is the worst. The area has become the greatest supplier of labour force. Agricultural products, such as, the jute, do not fetch remunerative prices. These are the common problems of entire North Bihar, and not only of the districts enumerated by Taslimuddin as part of the Seemanchal State demanded by him.

The area claimed has given many Chief Ministers to the State of Bihar, such as, Kedar Pandey, Jagannath Mishra, B.N. Mandal, Bhola Paswan Shastri, and Satish Prasad Sinha. Thus, the area produced the prominent political elites to take care of its developmental needs. Mr. Taslimuddin himself remained MLA for many terms. The area could not develop inspite of them.

The area claimed for the proposed State comes under many divisions of the State of Bihar, speaking different languages/dialects. The detail is given below:

Division	*Districts*	*Area (in sq. km.)*	*Population (1991)*	*Dialects Spoken*
Purnia	Purnia, Katihar, Araria, Kishanganj	15,733.4	62,95,695	Angika, Maithili, Kishanganjia
Koshi	Saharsa, Supaul, Madhepura	5,860.3	36,92,121	Angika, Maithili
Darbhanga	Darbhanga, Madhubani, Samastipur, Begusaria, Khagaria	12,087.0	1,08,52,965	Maithili, Angika
Tirhut	Sitamarhi, Purva Champaran, Pashchim Champaran	11,839.0	77,61,735	Bajjika, Bhojpuri, Maithili
Bhagalpur	Naugachhia subdivision of Bhagalpur district	Not Available	Not Available	Angika

Thus, the area claimed has about 46 thousand sq. kms. and three crore population. It may be mentioned that the area mentioned above minus two districts of Champaran form part of the 'Mithilanchal' claimed by its protagonists. Thus, there are overlapping demands in this case.

Md. Taslimuddin voiced his separatist demand five years ago in 1991, when he lost the Parliament election. He did it under the banner of the Kranti Morcha.[3] He subsequently won Assembly election in 1995 from Jokihat and became silent for some time.[4] Md. Taslimuddin and Mr. Rajesh Ranjan alias Pappu Yadav jointly addressed a meeting at Araria on September 4, 1995 and asked for the creation of the Seemanchal Development Council for 15 districts of Purnia, Koshi, Darbhanga and Tirhut divisions of North Bihar on the pattern of Jharkhand Area Development Council formed not even a month earlier.

Md. Taslimuddin formally launched the proposal for the Council at Kishanganj on September 13, 1995. The motive attributed for the move was to pressurise the Chief Minister to consider his candidature for the Janata Dal Ticket for the ensuing Lok Sabha elections. Mr. Pappu Yadav lost the Assembly election from Singheshwar and Purnia in 1995. The Purnia Lok Sabha election was countermanded in 1991. However, he won the Parliament seat in 1995. He wanted to keep Md. Taslimuddin happy to get the support of the Kulhaiya Muslim vote bank to ensure his victory in 1996 Parliament elections. He, therefore, joined hands with Taslimuddin to voice the demand for the Seemanchal Council.[5]

The creation of Jharkhand Area Autonomous Council generated hope in him and he voiced the demand for similar Council. He was emboldened to ask for Seemanchal State after the announcement of the creation of Uttarakhand.

The statehood demand for Seemanchal may not be easy to achieve due to following reasons:

(i) The area claimed is not compact. The communication network is very poor and this further aggravates the problem.

(ii) The demand for Mithilanchal and Seemanchal covers practically 90 per cent common area. The demand for Mithilanchal is an old demand and works in opposition to that of Seemanchal.

(iii) Purbi and Paschimi Champaran districts have greater affinities with Bhojpuri speaking Saran division. Similarly, Sitamarhi has more affinity with Bajjika speaking Muzaffarpur and Vaishali districts.

(iv) The parochial appeals of the Maithili, Bajjika, Bhojpuri and Angika languages and that of the Seemanchal do not work in consonance.

(v) Md. Taslimuddin does not have a clean image.

(vi) The creation of Seemanchal may accelerate the infiltration of Bangladeshis in the region.

(vii) The track record of mini-States is not satisfactory. They have failed to develop their respective areas inspite of heavy per capita plan expenditures.

(viii) Laloo Prasad Yadav and the Janata Dal oppose the move. The Janata Dal has the strongest mass-base in the area.

REFERENCES

1. *The Hindustan Times*, Patna, August 25, 1996, p. 1.
2. *Ibid.*
3. *Ibid.*
4. *Ibid.*
5. *Ibid.*

ANNEXURES

Constitutional Provision for the Formation of New States and Alteration of Boundaries

THERE is provision for the formation of new States and alteration of boundaries, etc. in the Constitution of India in the Articles 3 and 4. Article 3 says:

Parliament may by law—

(a) form a new State by separation of territory from any State or by uniting two or more States or parts of States or by uniting any territory to a part of any State;
(b) increase the area of any State;
(c) diminish the area of any State;
(d) alter the boundaries of any State;
(e) alter the name of any State.

[1][Provided that no Bill for the purpose shall be introduced in either House of Parliament except on the recommendation of the President and unless, where the proposal contained in the bill affects the area, boundaries or the name of any of the States[2]. . ., the Bill has been referred by the President to the Legislature of that State for expressing its views thereon within such period as may be specified in the reference or within such further period as the President may allow and the period so specified or allowed has expired.]

[3][*Explanation I*—In this article, in Clauses (a) to (e), "State" include a Union Territory, but in the proviso, "State" does not include a Union Territory.

Explanation II—The power conferred on Parliament by Clause (a) includes the power to form a new State or Union Territory by uniting a part of any State or Union Territory to any other State or Union Territory.]

Article 4

Laws made under Articles 2 and 3 to provide for the amendment of the First and the Fourth Schedules and supplemental, incidental and consequential matters—(1) Any Law referred to in Article 2 or Article

3 shall contain such provisions for the amendment of the First Schedule or the Fourth Schedule as may be necessary to give effect to the provisions of the Law and may also contain such supplemental, incidental and consequential provisions (including the provisions as to representation in Parliament and in the Legislature or Legislatures of the States affected by such Law) as Parliament may deem necessary.

(2) No such law as aforesaid shall be deemed to be an amendment of this Constitution for the purpose of Article 368.

REFERENCES

1. Substituted by the Constitution (Fifth Amendment) Act, 1955, s. 2 for the proviso.
2. The words and the letters "specified in Part A or Part B of the First Schedule" omitted by the Constitution (Seventh Amendment) Act, 1956, s. 29 and Schedule.
3. Inserted by the Constitution (Eighteenth Amendment) Act, 1966, s. 2.

The Area of the States and the Union Territories of India

States	Area (in sq. km.)	Percentage of the Total
Madhya Pradesh	4,43,446	13.49
Rajasthan	3,42,239	10.41
Maharashtra	3,07,690	9.36
Uttar Pradesh	2,94,411	8.96
Andhra Pradesh	2,75,068	8.37
Jammu & Kashmir	2,22,068	6.76
Gujarat	1,96,024	5.96
Karnataka	1,91,791	5.83
Bihar	1,73,877	5.29
Orissa	1,55,707	4.74
Tamil Nadu	1,30,058	3.96
West Bengal	88,752	2.70
Arunachal Pradesh	88,743	2.70
Assam	78,438	2.39
Himachal Pradesh	55,673	1.69
Punjab	50,362	1.53
Haryana	44,212	1.34
Kerala	38,863	1.18
Meghalaya	22,429	0.68
Manipur	22,327	0.68
Mizoram	21,081	0.64
Nagaland	16,579	0.50
Tripura	10,486	0.32
Sikkim	7,096	0.22
Goa	3,702	0.11
National Capital Territory		
Delhi	1,483	0.05
Union Territories		
Andaman & Nicobar Islands	8,249	0.25
Chandigarh	144	0.01
Dadra & Nagar Haveli	491	0.01
Daman & Diu	112	0.01
Lakshdweep	32	0.01
Pondicherry	492	0.01
Total—India	32,87,263	100.00

ANNEXURE-3

Population of the Indian States and Union Territories According to 1991 Census

State	*Population*	*Percentage of All-India Population*
Uttar Pradesh	13,87,60,417	16.44
Bihar	8,63,38,853	10.23
Maharashtra	7,87,06,719	9.33
West Bengal	6,79,82,732	8.06
Andhra Pradesh	6,63,04,854	7.86
Madhya Pradesh	6,61,35,862	7.84
Tamil Nadu	5,56,38,318	6.59
Karnataka	4,48,17,398	5.31
Rajasthan	4,38,80,640	5.20
Gujarat	4,11,74,060	4.88
Orissa	3,15,12,070	3.73
Kerala	2,90,11,237	3.44
Assam	2,22,94,562	2.64
Punjab	2,01,90,795	2.39
Haryana	1,63,17,715	1.93
Jammu & Kashmir	77,18,700	0.88
Himachal Pradesh	51,11,079	0.61
Tripura	27,44,827	0.32
Manipur	18,26,714	0.22
Meghalaya	17,60,626	0.21
Nagaland	12,15,573	0.14
Goa	11,68,622	0.14
Arunachal Pradesh	8,58,392	0.10
Mizoram	686,217	0.08
Sikkim	4,03,612	0.05
Delhi	93,70,475	1.11
Union Territories		
Pondicherry	7,89,416	0.09
Chandigarh	6,40,725	0.08
Andaman & Nicobar Islands	2,77,989	0.03
Dadra & Nagar Haveli	1,38,542	0.01
Daman & Diu	1,01,439	0.01
Lakshdweep	51,681	0.01
Total—India	84,39,30,861	100.00

Sources: 1. Census of India, 1991: Provisional Population Totals.
2. The 1991 Census was not conducted in Jammu & Kashmir. The Projected figures are prepared by the Standing Committee of Experts on Population Projections, 1989.

ANNEXURE-4

Subjects and the Departments under the Jurisdiction of Bodoland Autonomous Council

1. Cottage Industry
2. Animal Husbandry and Veterinary
3. Forests
4. Agriculture
5. PWD
6. Sericulture
7. Education
   (a) Adult Education
   (b) Primary Education
   (c) Upto Higher Secondary including Vocational Training
8. Cultural Affairs
9. Soil Conservation
10. Co-operation
11. Fisheries
12. Panchayat and Rural Development
13. Handloom and Textiles
14. Health and Family Welfare
15. Public Health Engineering
16. Irrigation
17. Social Welfare
18. Flood Control Schemes for Protection of Villages (not of highly technical nature)
19. Sports and Youth Welfare
20. Weights and Measures
21. Museums and Archaeology
22. Library Services
23. Urban Development—Town and Country Planning
24. Tribal Research Institute
25. College Education (General)
26. Land and Revenue
27. Publicity/Public Relations

28. Printing and Stationary
29. Tourism
30. Transport
31. Any other Matter Connected with Development
32. Municipal Corporation
    (a) Improvement Trusts
    (b) District Boards
    (c) Other Local Authorities
33. Tribal Welfare
34. Markets and Fairs
35. Lotteries, Theatres, Dramatic Performances
36. Vital Statistics including Registration of Births and Deaths
37. Intoxicating Liquors, Opium and Derivatives
38. Food and Civil Supply, etc.

Uttarakhand—Area and the Population of the Proposed State

District	*Area (in sq. km.)*	*Population (1991)*	*Headquarters*
Almora	5,385	8,24,134	Almora
Chamoli	9,125	4,41,667	Chamoli
Dehra Dun	3,088	10,14,700	Dehra Dun
Garhwal	5,397	6,66,165	Pauri
Nainital	6,794	15,57,415	Nainital
Pithoragarh	8,856	5,57,148	Pithoragarh
Tehri Garhwal	4,421	5,75,352	Narendranagar
Uttarkashi	8,016	2,37,772	Uttarkashi
Total	51,082	58,74,353	

Area and Population of the Jharkhand Region

State	*District*	*Area (in sq. km.)*	*Population (1991)*	*Headquarters*
Bihar	Deoghar	2,478.6	918,323	Deoghar
	Godda	2,110.4	858,678	Godda
	Sahibganj } Pakur }	3,405.4	1,297,391	Sahibganj
				Pakur
	Dumka	5,518.2	1,497,266	Dumka
	Dhanbad	2,996.0	2,709,170	Dhanbad
	Bokaro	3,342.6	14,47,870	Bokaro
	Hazaribagh } Kodarma }	7,458.8	2,376,174	Hazaribagh
				Koderma
	Giridih	6,892.0	2,224,006	Giridih
	Chatra	3,706.2	4,62,672	Chatra
	Palamu	8,704.9	1,844,289	Daltonganj
	Garhwa	4,044.1	6,06,759	Garhwa
	Ranchi	7,574.1	2,205,034	Ranchi
	Gumla	9,077.1	1,153,557	Gumla
	Lohardaga	1,490.9	288,585	Lohardaga
	Purbi-Singhbhum	3,533.3	1,617,170	Jamshedpur
	Pashchimi-Singhbhum	8,012.0	1,789,796	Chaibasa
	Total	80,344.6	2,32,98,740	
Madhya Pradesh	Surguja	22,337	2,082,930	Ambikapur
	Raigarh	12,924	1,724,420	Raigarh
	Total	35,261	38,07,350	
West Bengal	Bankura	6,882.0	2,799,455	Bankura
	Midnapore	14,081.0	8,349,890	Midnapore
	Total	20,963.0	11,149,345	
Orissa	Sudargarh	9,942	1,568,442	Sundargarh
	Sambalpur } Tharsuguda } Deogada }	11,689	1,484,765	Sambalpur
				Tharsugada
				Deogada
	Mayurbhanja	10,412	1,871,796	Baripara
	Keonjhar	8,240	13,15,627	Keonjhar
	Total	40,283	62,40,630	
	Grand Total	1,76,841.6	4,44,96,065	

ANNEXURE-7

Area and Population of Telangana Region

District	*Area (in sq. km.)*	*Population (1991)*	*Headquarters*
Adilabad	16,128	2,080,231	Adilabad
Hyderabad	217	3,091,718	Hyderabad
Ranga Reddy	7,493	2,528,208	Hyderabad
Karimnagar	11,823	3,043,228	Karimnagar
Khammam	16,029	2,200,081	Khammam
Mahboob Nagar	18,432	3,071,765	Mahaboob Nagar
Medak	9,699	2,264,124	Sangareddy
Nalgonda	14,240	2,850,183	Nalgonda
Nizamabad	7,956	2,034,794	Nizamabad
Warrangal	12,846	2,811,174	Warrangal
Total	1,14,863	2,59,75,506	

ANNEXURE-8

Vidarbha Region of Maharashtra

District	*Area (in sq. km.)*	*Population (1991)*	*Headquarters*
Buldhana	9,661	1,881,438	Buldhana
Akola	10,575	2,211,016	Akola
Amarawati	12,212	2,206,562	Amarawati
Yavatmal	13,584	2,073,708	Yavatmal
Wardha	6,310	1,085,589	Wardha
Nagpur	9,931	3,274,974	Nagpur
Bhandara	9,213	2,103,276	Bhandara
Chandrapur	10,490	1,768,945	Chandrapur
Gadchiroli	15,433	785,626	Gadchiroli
Total	97,409	1,73,91,134	

Mithilanchal—The Area and the Population Claimed by the Protagonists

District	*Area (in sq. km.)*	*Population (1991)*	*Headquarters*
Sitamarhi } Shivahar }	2,643.0	23,88,822	Sitamarhi Shivahar
Muzaffarpur	3,172	29,46,601	Muzaffarpur
Vaishali	2,036	21,44,252	Hajipur
Begusarai	1,918.0	18,13,214	Begusarai
Samastipur	2,904.0	27,15,297	Samastipur
Darbhanga	2,279.0	25,09,083	Darbhanga
Madhubani	3,501.0	28,28,640	Madhubani
Saharsa	2,814.4	18,95,956	Saharsa
Madhepura	1,788.5	11,78.060	Madhepura
Supaul	1,257.4	6,18,105	Supaul
Purnia	7,943.0	18,76,287	Purnia
Katihar	3,057.0	18,21,590	Katihar
Araria	2,794.9	16,11,145	Araria
Kishanganj	1,938.5	9,86,672	Kishanganj
Khagaria	1,485.8	9,86,731	Khagaria
Bhagalpur	2,568.8	21,59,797	Bhagalpur
Godda	2,110.4	8.58,678	Godda
Banka	3,020.2	10,38,674	Banka
Deoghar	2,478.6	9,18,323	Deoghar

Note: (i) The area claimed in Bihar roughly corresponds to the area shown above. This includes some Bajjika language areas, such as, Muzaffarpur, Sitamarhi, Vaishali, etc.; Angika language area, such as Bhagalpur, Banka, Khagaria, Katihar, etc.; and Deoghar and Godda included in the Jharkhand Autonomous Area.

(ii) Mr. Taslimuddin has voiced the demand for the creation of "Simanchal" State consisting of the frontier districts of Purnia, Araria, Kishanganj, Katihar, Madhepura, Saharsa, Supaul, Khagaria, Naugachhia (part of Bhagalpur district), Madhubani, Sitamarhi, Darbhanga, East Champaran and West Champaran. All the districts mentioned above except the last two form part of the list given above. This shows considerable overlap in the State demands.

ANNEXURE-10

Autonomy Demand within the State of Jammu & Kashmir

District	*Area (in sq. km.)*	*Population (1991)*	*Headquarters*
Jammu Region			
Jammu	3,097	9,43,395	Jammu
Udhampur	4,550	4,53,636	Udhampur
Doda	11,691	4,25,262	Doda
Poonch	1,674	2,24,197	Punch
Rajauri	2,630	3,02,500	Rajouri
Kathua	2,651	3,69,123	Rajouri
Total	26,293	27,18,113	
Ladakh Region			
Ladakh	82,665	68,380	Leh
Kargil	14,036	55,992	Kargil
Total	96,701	1,24,372	

Note: The area of Ladakh shown above includes 37,555 sq. km. illegally occupied by China.

(i) Estimated population is shown above as no census was taken in Jammu & Kashmir during 1991.

Regions of Madhya Pradesh Demanding Statehood

State	*District*	*Area (in sq. km.)*	*Population (1991)*	*Headquarters*
Chattisgarh	Raipur	21,558	39,08,042	Raipur
	Surguja	22,337	9,40,609	Ambikapur
	Durg	8,537	23,98,497	Durg
	Rajnandgaon	11,127	14,39,951	Rajnandgaon
	Raigarh	6,154	9,92,764	Raigarh
	Bilaspur	19,897	37,96,553	Bilaspur
	Bastar	39,114	22,70,472	Jagdalpur
	Total	1,28,724	1,57,26,888	
Bundelkhand	Chatarpur	8,687	11,58,853	Chatarpur
	Tikamgarh	5,048	9,40,609	Tikamgarh
	Shivpuri	10,278	11,31,933	Shivpuri
	Gwalior	5,214	14,14,948	Gwalior
	Datia	2,038	3,97,743	Datia
	Bhind	4,459	12,14,480	Bhind
	Total	35,724	62,58,566	

Note: (i) Jashpur subdivision of Raigarh district does not come under Chattisgarh.
(ii) Parts of the above-mentioned regions fall under Uttar Pradesh.
(iii) There is mild demands for separate State in other parts of the State also.

Bundelkhand Region of U.P. :

District	*Area (in sq. km.)*	*Population (1991)*	*Headquarters*
Banda	7,624	18,51,014	Banda
Hamirpur	7,165	14,65,401	Hamirpur
Jalaun	4,565	12,17,021	Orai
Jhansi	5,024	14,26,721	Jhansi
Lalitpur	5,039	7,48,997	Lalitpur
Total	29,417	67,09,154	

State Autonomy Demands in Assam

The Hill State

District	*Area (in sq. km.)*	*Population (1991)*	*Headquarters*
Karbi Anglong	10,332	6,55,415	Diphu
North Cachar Hills	4,890	1,49,346	Haflong
Total	15,222	8,04,761	

Cachar

District	*Area (in sq. km.)*	*Population (1991)*	*Headquarters*
Cachar	5,102.2	12,15,952	Silchar
Karimganj	1,839.0	8,25,551	Karimganj
Hailakandi	1,326.1	4,48,506	Hailakandi
Total	8,267.3	24,90,009	

BIBLIOGRAPHY

Barpujari, H.K., *Problems of Hill Tribes: North-East Frontier*, Gauhati, United Publications.

Basic Statistics of North-Eastern Region, 1992, Shillong, North-Eastern Council Secretariat, 1992.

Basnet, Lal Bahadur, *Sikkim: A Short Political History*, New Delhi, S. Chand & Company, 1978.

Bose Manilal, *Historical and Constitutional Documents of North-Eastern India (1824-1973)*, Delhi, Concept, 1979.

Census of India, Series 3, Assam, Part I-A, 1971.

Census of India 1991, Series-1, Paper-2 of 1992, Final Population Totals; Brief Analysis of Primary Census Abstracts.

Chaube, S.K., *Hill Politics in North-East India*, Calcutta, Orient Longman, 1973.

Dubey, S.M. (ed.), *North-East India: A Sociological Study*, Delhi, Concept, 1978.

Datta, P.S., *North-East and the Indian State, Paradoxes of a Periphery*, New Delhi, Vikash, 1995.

———, *Autonomy Movements in Assam* (Documents), New Delhi, Omsons, 1993.

Gait, Sir Edward Albert, *History of Assam*, Guwahati, Lawyers Book Stall, 6th edition, 1994.

Gan Chaudhuri, Jagadis, *A Political History of Tripura*, New Delhi, Inter-India Publications, 1985.

Grover, B.L., S. Grover, *A New Look at Modern Indian History*, Delhi, S. Chand & Company Ltd., 1995.

Kashmir Special, *Aaj* (Hindi), Patna, April 18, 1993.

Kumar, B.B., *Re-organization of North-East India* (Facts and Documents), New Delhi, Omsons, 1996.

———, *Trends of British Annexation of North-East India,* New Delhi, Omsons, 1994.

———, *Modernization in Naga Society*, New Delhi, Omsons, 1993.

———, *Tension and Conflict in North-East India,* New Delhi, Cosmo, 1995.

Luthra, P.N., Nagaland, *From a District to a State*, Shillong, Director, Information and Public Relations, Arunachal Pradesh, 1974.

Mahajan, V.D., *India Since 1526*, New Delhi, S. Chand & Company Ltd., 1996.

Majumdar, R.C., Raychaudhuri, H.C., Datta, Kalikinkar, *An Advanced History of India,* Macmillan, 1978.

Manorama Yearbook 1995.

Mackenzie, A., *The North-East Frontier of India*, Delhi, Mittal Publications, Reprint, 1981.

Prasad, R.N. (ed.), *Political and Economic Development of Mizoram*, New Delhi, Mittal, 1991.

———, *Autonomy Movements in Mizoram*, New Delhi, Vikas, 1994.

Rao, V. Venkata, *Century of Government and Politics in North-East India*, New Delhi, S. Chand & Company, Vol. I—Assam, 1983; Vol. II—Meghalaya, 1984; Vol. III—Mizoram, 1987; Vol. IV—Manipur, 1991.

Roy Chaudhury, P.C., *Gazetteer of India: Bihar, Purnea, Patna*, 1963.

The Report of the States Reorganization Commission, 1956.

Singh, Chandrika, *Emergence of Arunachal Pradesh as a State*, New Delhi, Mittal, 1989.

Singh, K. Suresh, *People of India, Sikkim,* Anthropological Survey of India/Sea Gull Books, Calcutta, 1993.

Singh, Prakash, *Nagaland*, New Delhi, National Book Trust, 1972.

Sinha, Awadhesh Coomar, *Politics of Sikkim: Sociological Study*, Faridabad, Thomson, 1975.

Sinha, Kamaleshwar, Meghalaya: *Triumph of the Tribal Genius*, Delhi, Publications Division (ISSD), 1970.

Stracey, P.D., *Nagaland Nightmare*, New Delhi, Allied Publications, 1968.

The Constitution of India, Delhi, Govt. of India.

Papers

Chakraborty, Tapas, Dems Unscrupulous, *The Telegraph*, June 28, 1995.

Jagmohan, Autonomy of Kashmir, Jagmohan on its pitfalls, *The Hindustan Times*, August 15, 1996.

John Varkey, Bobby, States on a Platter, *The Hindustan Times*, Sunday Magazine, September 8, 1996.

Kumar, B.B., North-East India: Need for a Fresh Look, *The Administrator*, Vol. XXXIX, No. 4, October-December 1994; also in *North-East and the Indian State: Paradoxes of a Periphery*, P.S. Datta, New Delhi, Vikas.

_______, Insurgency in North-East India: Some Reflections, in B. Pakem, *Insurgency in North-East India*, New Delhi, Omsons.

Nayar, Kuldip, Smaller States Okay, but . . ., *The Hindustan Times*, September 1, 1996.

Re-mapping the Country, *India Today*, October 15, 1996.

Rajeshwar, T.V., Now Reap the Whirlwind, *The Hindustan Times*, September, 6, 1996.

Singh, Amar Kumar, Tough Tasks, Horny Tests, *The Hindustan Times*, Monday Extra, August 14, 1996.

Singh, K. Khogen, Bodos Still Chasing an Illusive Autonomy, *The Hindustan Times*, May 7, 1995.

Stobdan, P., Mishandling Ladakh may Prove Costly, *The Times of India*, Patna, April 5, 1995.

Srivastava, N.M.P., Recreating History, *The Hindustan Times*, Monday Extra, April 1, 1996.

Will JAAC Spell Change?, *The Hindustan Times*, Monday Extra, August 7, 1996.

Editorials

Mr. Pilot On Barpeta, The Sentinel, Gauhati, July 29, 1994.

Setback to Jharkhand, The Hindustan Times, July 2, 1996.

Materials Used/quoted mostly from

Aaj (Hindi)
Frontline,
India Today,
The Times of India,
The Hindustan Times,
The Telegraph,
The Sentinel,
The Assam Tribune,
The North East Times,
The Shillong Times,
The Tribune.

INDEX

Adivasis Council, 108
Administrative systems, 17
Agitations, 24, 54, 102, 124, 154
 present phase of, 85
Aggressive minoritism, 21-23
Akhil Bharatiya Gorkha League (ABGL), 93, 95, 99
All-Bodo Students Union (ABSU), 104, 106, 112
All-India Congress Committee, 39, 52
All-Jharkhand Students Union (AJSU), 117, 118
All-Party Hill Leaders Conference (APHLC), 50, 68, 69, 70, 71, 72, 76, 150
Ambedkar, B.R., 18, 39, 83, 143
Anchal Samities, 78
Anglo-Sikh, 30
Annie Besant, 52
Arunachal Pradesh, 78, 79, 80
Assam,
 bulkamisation of, 61
 state autonomy demand, 176
Assam Chah Mazdur Sangh (ACMS), 109
Assam Disturbed Area Act, 1955, 74
Assam Gana Parishad, 109, 153
Assam Legislative Assembly, 24
Autonomous Area Council Experiments, 23
Autonomous District Councils, 20
Autonomous State Demand Committee (ASDC), 153
Autonomous State of Meghalaya, 50
Autonomy, 17, 21, 103
Azad Chhatisgarh Fauz, 131

Bahuguna, H.N., 83
Baluchistan, 31
Bangladesh, 143
 immigrants, 110
Basant Sathe, 138
Battle of Plassey, 29
Bengal Presidency, 30
Bhandari, Nar Bhahadur, 92, 93, 94, 99
Bharatiya Janata Party (BJP), 86, 99, 119, 131, 133, 138
Bhojpuri speaking areas, 148
Bihar, 28, 29, 30
Bihar Legislative Assembly, 116
Biharis, 30
Black-flag demonstration, 55
Bodos, 20
 language, 101
 population, 103
 reaction of, 109
Bodo Sahitya Sabha, 105, 112
Bodoland, 87
 demands for, 17
 movement, 103
 unending conflict in, 101-110
Bodoland Autonomous Council (BAC), 22, 23, 106, 108, 109, 111
 area armed activities, 109-110
 jurisdiction of, 167-68
Bordolai, Gopi Nath, 18
Bordolai Committee, 47
Boundaries, alteration of, 163-65
Brahma, Gurudev Kalicharan, 101, 104
Bhahma, Prem Singh, 111, 112
British Council functionaries, 18
British colonial policy, 17
British-Indian provinces, 29
British paramountcy, 32, 36
Bundhs, 24, 105, 153, 154
Bundelkhand, 129
 area and population, 175
 districts of, 133
Butler Committee, 18
 recommendations, 37
Cabinet Mission, 38, 39
Civil disobedience movement, 63
Committee on Jharkhand Matters (COJM), 118
Consolidated Fund of India, 24, 61, 73, 74, 102
Constitutional provisions, 163-64

Coordinations Committee for Leh Autonomous Council (CCLAC), 125
Corruption, 19
Coupland Plan, 18

Darjeeling, 91
    states of, 95-96
Darjeeling Autonomous Gorkha Hill Council, 23, 86, 92, 95, 125
Delhi agreement, 143
Deve Gowda, H.D., 15, 24, 99, 146
Dhar Committee, 53
Dharnas, 108, 133
District Council, 48, 49
    functioning of, 50
    power of, 50
District Level Autonomy, 47-51

East India Company, 29, 34, 35
Eastern Hill State, 66
    agenda of, 66
    demand for, 50
Edwardes, Michael, 55
Elections, 23
Exploitation, 20, 21
1857 Sepoy Mutiny, 17, 18

Federal Plan, 71
Firman, 43

Gairsain, 87
Gait, Edward, 102
Gorkha National Liberation Front (GNLF), 92, 94
Gorkhaland,
    agitation, 102
    demands for, 17, 93
    imbroglio, 91-100
Gorkhaland People's Front (GPF), 99

Hawala, 102
Hill State Demand, 66
Hindu majority provinces, 31
Hutton, J.P., 60
Hyderabad, 93

Identity crisis, problems of, 20
Illegal immigrants, 111
Indira Gandhi, 104
Indo-Bhutan Treaty, 96
Indo-Nepal Treaty, 98
Indo-Pakistan War, 43
Indo-Sikkim Treaty, 79
Industrialisation, 157
Inner-line regulation, 59
Instrument of Accession, 40, 43

Jagannath Mishra, 118, 146, 157
Jaipal Reddy S., 136
Jaipal Singh, 113, 117
Jammu & Kashmir, 44, 122, 125
    autonomy demand, 174
    perception differences, 143-44
    population, 141
Jammu & Ladakh,
    discrimination, 144-45
Janata Dal, 119, 136, 138, 148
Jawaharlal-Vallabhai Patel-Pattabhi Sitarammiya Committee, 52
Jharkhand, 20, 87, 103
    area and population of, 113, 170
    bundh, 118
    demands for, 16
    movement, 113-16
        characteristics of, 116-17
    separation of, 146
Jharkhand Area Autonomous Council (JAAC), 22, 23, 119, 120, 121, 158
Jharkhand Mukti Morch, 117
Jinnah, 41, 42, 63
Judicial activism, 19
Junagarh, 40, 43
Jyoti Basu, 92, 93, 94

Kakatiya University, 136
Kalyan Singh, 94
Karbi-Anglong,
    statehood demand, 150-54
Karbi-Anglong North Cachar Hills Autononous State Demand Committee (KANCHADCOM), 153
Kasim Rizvi, 44
Kashmiri leaders, 124
Kathiawad, 34, 40
Khalistan, 93
Koch-Rajbansis, 22
    community, 108
Kranti Morcha, 158

Kshatriya, 22
Kumar, B.B., 32

Ladakh,
  autonomy movement, 124
  demand for, 17
Ladakh Autonomous Hill Council, 122
Ladakh-Buddhist Association, 124
Ladakh Leh Hill Council, 23
Ladakhis, 122, 124
Lakshman Jha, 148
Lal Denga, 74, 75, 78
Laloo Prasad Yadav, 94, 118, 119, 148, 157
Lalthanhawala, 77
Language speaking problem, 53
Lee-Warner, William, 34
Left Front Ministry, 92
Leh Autonomous Hill Council, 145
Linguistic Provinces Committee, 53
Linguistic Reorganisation, 52-60
Linguistic States, 20, 53-54
Lord Canning, 35
Lord Dalhousie, 34
Lord Hardinge, 30
Lord Mountbatten, 40, 43, 44
Low-Sky state demands, 129-40
LTTE, 93

Mackenzie, 95, 96
Madhya Pradesh Demanding Statehood, 175
Mahanta, Prafulla Kumar, 109
Maharashtrawadi Gomantaka Dal, 62
Mahatma Gandhi, 52, 53, 59
Malwa, demand for, 140
Mandal, B.N., 157
Manipur, 22, 25, 74
Mayurbhanj joined Orissa, 40
Meghalaya, 66, 67, 91, 101, 150
  autonomous states of, 72
Mehta Plan, 71, 150
Mikir Hills Progressive Party, 150, 157
Mithila state,
  demand for, 146-150
Mithilanchal, 158
  area and population, 173
Mithilanchal Vikash Congress, 148
Mizos, 74, 75, 77
Mizo National Front (MNF), 75, 76
  memorandum, 76
  propaganda, 75
Mizoram, 74
Montagu-Chelmsford Reform, 52, 59
Morarji Desai, 88
Motilal Vora, 86
Mufti Muhammad Said, 144
Mulayam Singh, 85
Muslim League, 40
Muslim majority provinces, 31, 54
Muzaffarpur incident, 85

Naga Hills, autonomy movement, 60
Naga problems, 18
Naga National Council (NNC), 62, 63
Naga People's Convention, 64, 65
Nagaland, 24, 59, 152
  creation of, 55
  demand for, 65
Nanda Committee, recommendations of, 71-72
Narasimha Rao, P.V., 119
Nawab of Bhopal, 42
Naxalities, 121
Negotiations, 44
Nehru, Jawaharlal, 55, 69, 88, 143
Nehru Plan, 70
Nepali Bhasha Samity, 93, 94
New states
  formation of, 163-63
New Testament, 45
Nizam, 44
Nizam of Hyderabad, 42
Non-Bodo Villages, 108
North-Cachar hills, 150
North-East Frontier Agency Panchayat Raj Regulation, 78
North-Eastern (Re-organization) Act, 78, 79
North-Eastern Hills,
  separation of, 59

Official Languages Bill, 68
Orissa, 29, 30, 31, 41
Other Backward Castes (OBC), 86
Oudh, 29

Pakistan, 17, 31, 45, 63, 143
  overtures, 41-42
  separation of, 63

Panchayat elections, 23, 95
Pannikar, K.M., 87, 88
Pant, G.B., 83, 88
Pappu Yadav, 185
Paramountcy, 39
Partition, 17
Pataskar Commission, 50, 71, 150
Patel, Sardar Valabhbhai, 18, 40, 47
Pending state demands, 129-30
Phizo, A.Z., 62, 63
Plains Tribal Council of Assam (PTCA), 104
Policy lapses, 111
Political culture, 25
Political organization,
 growth of, 104-105
Post-reform development, 36-37
Poverty alleviation programmes, 19
Princely states,
 merger of, 38-50
Punjab, 31, 41
Punjabi suba, 54, 57
Purnia Lok Sabha election, 158

Queens proclamation, 35

Radcliff Award, 45
Rail Roko agitation, 153
Rajputana, 34
Rajesh Pilot, 106, 138
Ramaswami Aiyar, C.P., 42
Rational Parameters, 23
Regional Councils, 48
Ring Fence Policy, 34
Robert Neil Reid, 18, 59
Roy, B.M., 66
Royal proclamation, 36

Sanad, 32, 33, 35
Sangma, Williamson, 66
Santal Pargana Swadeshi Parishad, 120
Santal tribes, 22
Scottish Plan, 69
Second World War, 60, 64
Securing autonomy, 102
Seemanchal Development Council, 158
Seemanchal State,
 demands for, 140, 157
 recent demand for, 149, 159
Separate State Demand Committee, 152
Shastri, Bhola Paswan, 157
Sheikh Abdullah, 45, 122, 124, 143, 144
Shiv Sena, 138
Sibu Soren, 116, 117, 119
Simon Commission, 104
 report, 59
Singh, V.P., 99
Sinha, Sachchidanand, 30
Sitaram Kesari, 138
Sixth Schedule, 47,
 autonomy, 150
 constitutional provision, 75
 extension of the provision, 49-50
Small states merged, 40
Small states demands, 20-21
 syndrome, 59-64
Social activism, 25
Soft state syndrome, 109, 110
Sovereignty, declaration of, 42-43
Stand-still agreement, 42, 43, 45
States demands, 17
 categories of, 45-46
States Union, 40
State's Reorganization Commission, 54, 66, 78, 83, 89, 117
 memorandum to, 66
 recommendations, 56-57
Strecey, P.D., 55
Subhas Ghising, 91, 92, 93, 94, 95, 96, 98, 99
Sultan Shuja, 29
Suraj Mandal, 119

Taslimuddin, 157, 158, 159
Tea gardens, 109
Telangana, 129, 133
 area and population, 171
 separation of, 136
Telugu Desam Party, 136
Thinker Politicians, 15
Tilak, Balgangadhar, 52
Tiwari, N.D., 73, 133
Tribal courts, 21
 league, 104
Tripura, 74

Udayanchal, 104
ULFA, 93
Uma Bharati, 133
Union States, 40

Union Territories,
    area of states, 165-66
    population, 166
United Front Government, 15
United Nationalist Organisation, 152
United provinces, 29-30
Uttarakhand, 15, 133, 138
    area and population, 169
    creation of, 159
    districts consists of, 83
    movement, 85
    statehood of, 83-88
Uttarakhand Kranti Dal (UKD), 85
Uttar Pradesh, 87
    bifurcation of, 88

Viceroy, 36, 42
Vidarbha, 129
    area and population, 172
    districts of, 136-37
    regions of, 137
    state demand for, 138
Vidarbha Rajya Sanghursh Samiti, 138
Village Council, 78
Village Panchayat, 118
Vishnu Purana, 97
Vote Bank considerations, 25

West Bengal, 31
West Bengal Border, 157

Zilla Parishad, 78